What Men

WITH ASPERGER SYNDROME

Want to Know

About Women, Dating
and Relationships

by the same author

The Asperger Couple's Workbook
Practical Advice and Activities for Couples and Counsellors
Maxine Aston
ISBN 978 1 84310 253 3
eISBN 978 1 84642 851 7

Aspergers in Love
Maxine Aston
Foreword by Gisela Slater-Walker
ISBN 978 1 84310 115 4
eISBN 978 1 84642 394 9

of related interest

22 Things a Woman with Asperger's Syndrome Wants
Her Partner to Know
Rudy Simone
Foreword by Tony Attwood
ISBN 978 1 84905 883 4
eISBN 978 0 85700 586 1

22 Things a Woman Must Know If She Loves a Man
with Asperger's Syndrome
Rudy Simone
Foreword by Maxine Aston
ISBN 978 1 84905 803 2
eISBN 978 1 84642 945 3

What Men

WITH ASPERGER SYNDROME

Want to Know

About Women, Dating and Relationships

MAXINE ASTON

Foreword by Tony Attwood
Illustrated by William Z. Aston

Jessica Kingsley *Publishers*
London and Philadelphia

First published in 2012
by Jessica Kingsley Publishers
73 Collier Street
London N1 9BE, UK
and
400 Market Street, Suite 400
Philadelphia, PA 19106, USA

www.jkp.com

Library of Congress Cataloging in Publication Data
Aston, Maxine C.
  What men with asperger syndrome want to know about women, dating and
relationships / Maxine
Aston ; foreword by Tony Attwood.
    p. cm.
  Includes bibliographical references.
  ISBN 978-1-84905-269-6 (alk. paper)
  1. Asperger's syndrome--Patients--Family relationships. 2. Interpersonal
communication. 3. Man-
woman relationships. I. Title.
  RC553.A88A48835 2012
  616.85'8832--dc23

2012009487

British Library Cataloguing in Publication Data
A CIP catalogue record for this book is available from the British Library

ISBN 978 1 84905 269 6
eISBN 978 0 85700 554 0

Printed and bound in the United States

Dedicated to my father,
the late William E. Aston 1920–1989

You are the bravest man I have ever known
You looked Death in the eyes
You held him in your powerful hands
And decided when to die.

Contents

AND THEN THERE WERE THREE...   173

Foreword

When I conduct a comprehensive diagnostic assessment for Asperger syndrome, one of the factors I am trying to determine is whether or not either parent shows characteristics of the syndrome. In about half of the families I have seen, there are subtle signs within one parent: usually, but not exclusively, the father. In current colloquial parlance, when it comes to the genetic predisposition for Asperger syndrome, 'the apple does not fall far from the tree'; in other words, one of the causes of Asperger syndrome is the inheritance and amplification of specific traits. This leads to the intriguing conclusion that over the centuries, people must have fallen in love with partners who have characteristics of Asperger syndrome in order to maintain the current prevalence of autism spectrum disorders (ASDs). This prevalence has recently been estimated by the Centers for Disease Control and Prevention as one child in 88 (Centers for Disease Control and Prevention 2012). Thus, it seems that falling in love with someone with the characteristics of Asperger syndrome is a relatively common occurrence.

There must be advantages to having ASD in the gene pool. I suspect that significant advances in science and the arts have been achieved by people who have the characteristics of Asperger syndrome. If this is so, then we need Aspies (the endearing term to describe someone who has Asperger syndrome). It follows, then, that Aspies must have characteristics appealing to a partner. What are those characteristics?

In conversations with parents, and when conducting workshops for partners, I have noted a number of recurring qualities. These include: knowledge and intellect; artistic and literary talents; a unique perspective in problem solving; confidence about opinions; kindness and thoughtfulness; attention to detail; and good career prospects. Other appealing characteristics, especially in the initial stages of the relationship, can be the tendency to have a 'Peter Pan' quality – for example, still avidly collecting train sets, to have had few previous relationships and associated relationship 'baggage', being good-looking and attentive, and having shared intellectual interests. The diagnostic characteristic of Asperger syndrome of being confused or overwhelmed in social situations can elicit strong maternal or caring instincts in a potential partner (sometimes this characteristic is recognised in a relative, especially a much-loved parent). I have noticed that when someone falls in love with a person who has the characteristics of Asperger syndrome, the depth of love and commitment can be the greatest that person has ever experienced.

What does a man with Asperger syndrome seek in his partner? There may be two types of women attractive for and attracted to a man with Asperger syndrome. One type (the minority) have very similar abilities and characteristics to their Aspie partners. They are like-minded in terms of social and emotional needs, both enjoying periods of solitude, with conversation being primarily to exchange information rather than feelings. They may have the same careers and hobbies and expectations in a relationship. This group are less likely to need or seek relationship counselling.

The other type, who are the majority, have qualities of being nurturing and compassionate, with a natural maternal instinct. They are often gregarious with an established circle of friends, and are able to act as a social interpreter and guide for the man with Asperger syndrome. Such women are also able to naturally and easily reassure and calm their partner, who may have intense emotions, especially anxiety and anger. They are usually women who have a great capacity to express and enjoy affection and compassion towards family and friends. I describe such individuals as being 'extreme neurotypical': the other end of the social understanding continuum to those who have Asperger syndrome.

After the initial intoxicating romance between the man with Asperger syndrome and this latter type of woman, there can be a gradual realisation from both partners that the relationship is not as fulfilling as anticipated. There then follows a grieving process for the relationship that did not materialise. Both partners will progress through the grieving process, but at different rates, often with the neurotypical partner progressing at a faster rate. The first stage is disbelief, with a reluctance to acknowledge what may be very apparent to friends and family members. This phase can take many years before realisation dawns that the relationship is moving in a direction that both partners find increasingly difficult to accept. The extreme neurotypical woman may have made more adjustments to make than her Aspie partner, for example, reducing the frequency and duration of social experiences that she finds enthralling and energising because her partner finds social gatherings exhausting and pointless. He may appear to achieve more enjoyment from solitude and being engaged in a special interest than spending time in conversation at home. The conversations that do occur can be superficial and brief, with the Aspie partner having difficulty expressing his inner thoughts, feelings and experiences. He may struggle to notice, recall or even want to talk about information of emotional significance for the neurotypical partner. She starts to feel neglected and lonely.

One of the characteristics of Asperger syndrome can be a difficulty in expressing love and affection in the ways anticipated by a neurotypical partner, who needs daily verbal and tactile expressions of affection. She can feel deprived of the degree of affection she needs and this will affect her self-esteem and mood. She may find it hard to cope with her partner's chronic anxiety and associated perfectionism and routines, his explosive rages over minor irritations, and his not being able to resonate with her euphoria in social situations and her desire to sometimes be frivolous and silly. Aspects of the relationship that were appealing during the courtship phase can become irritating, with the extreme neurotypical woman now accusing her partner of being arrogant, pedantic, critical, deflating and immature. She may resent the person she has become, feeling she is expected to be a replacement mother with unconditional acceptance and support. She may go through a personality change, and start to 'mirror' the characteristics of her Aspie partner, adopting the same value system, lifestyle and thinking, simply in order to survive with a partner who resists being changed. The characteristics seem 'infectious' from Aspie to neurotypical, but not necessarily the other way round (which was what she had hoped would happen in the relationship). There can also be elements of co-dependency, such that she has to micromanage her Aspie partner's daily life. This can be exhausting, especially since there is little appreciation of the sacrifices she is making. Eventually, there is the recognition by the extreme neurotypical woman that the relationship is not flourishing, and the second stage of grieving is reached.

The Aspie partner can also, but usually more gradually, consider the relationship to be not what he anticipated. During the courtship phase he will have great motivation to be a successful partner, but little intuitive knowledge and experience in how to be one, according to modern expectations. The Aspie partner may have had few friends during his childhood and adolescence and been a late developer in terms of romantic experiences. Thus, he may have limited knowledge of relationships, especially aspects such as understanding and accepting an alternative perspective and priorities, constructively managing conflict and making compromises, and sharing responsibilities to achieve a balanced partnership. He becomes increasingly aware of not fulfilling the social, emotional, conversational and intimacy needs of his neurotypical partner. He unintentionally makes mistakes in what to do or say and feels criticised for being who he is. He may receive increasingly less guidance in what is expected, being told, 'Well, you should know, how long have we lived together?' The Aspie partner can find maintaining a successful relationship an increasingly complex problem, with no 'operator's manual' to understand how to make his partner happy or how to live with someone who seems moody, irrational, emotionally volatile and obsessed with daily expressions of affection, and being told she is attractive and appreciated. He has difficulty living with someone who does not understand the importance of logic over emotion, or appreciate that his special interest is a source of intense enjoyment, often superior to any interpersonal or intimate experience. It provides an escape from a complex world with so many social demands, and creates a sense of identity and expertise. To be asked to dispose of components of a special interest in the belief that they are clutter is akin to asking the neurotypical to discard a photo album. His attempts to correct (and 'improve') his partner as she goes about her household activities and routines are rejected. They experience very different priorities and pleasures in life. The Aspie begins to feel he is a relationship failure.

The second stage for both partners in the grieving process is the experience of intense emotions. The extreme neurotypical and the Aspie can feel powerful anger and frustration at being thwarted in achieving the relationship that was anticipated. This can lead to arguments, accusations and temporary separations, and can contribute to a decision to finally end the relationship. That is not an easy decision, especially knowing that the Aspie partner may have difficulty coping emotionally and practically on his own, and that the neurotypical partner may become a single parent. It is important to note, however, that the energy created by anger can be used constructively to seek counselling and mutual understanding. The other emotion is despair which, in the long term, evolves into a clinical depression. This depression can deprive either partner of the energy and motivation to change the relationship. The chronic stress and disappointment can affect mental as well as physical health. This stage could last decades or the duration of the relationship.

However, most importantly, there is a third possible stage, namely the accommodation and appreciation by both partners of their differences, and their mutual willingness to change, learn and enjoy each other's qualities; to use Maxine's terminology, not to leave it or lump it, but to like it. This book provides information and wisdom on how someone with Asperger syndrome can achieve, maintain and enjoy a successful long-term relationship. The content resonates with my experience of supporting and guiding so many adults with Asperger syndrome seeking a partner or requesting relationship counselling, from a couple who have only recently fallen in love to those who have been together for decades and become grandparents. If you have Asperger syndrome or are in a relationship with someone who has Asperger syndrome this book will change your life for the better.

Tony Attwood
Minds & Hearts Clinic
Brisbane, Australia

Acknowledgements

A big thank you to all the men who have trusted me to support them and help them make sense of the complex and confusing world of women and relationships. For you this book is written.

Thank you, Professor Tony Attwood, for writing the foreword for this book and for your continued genuine support and inspiration.

Thank you to all who have offered me their support over the years, including Jason Thompson, Karen Rodman, Katrin Bentley, Harriet Simons, Rudy Simone and a lady called 'Anonymous'.

Thank you, Zoe, for giving me your precious time as a busy mother to read through the book and make some valuable suggestions.

Thank you, William, for drawing the sketches and giving me the benefit of your sense of humour.

Thank you, Peter, for, as always, offering me advice, guidance and the benefit of your most unique mind.

Thank you to my friend Georgina Blake-Hall for the time you spent proofreading my work; you are an angel in disguise.

A special thank you to Paulette, my beautiful brave sister, who offered some ideas of her own.

Thank you to my children and their partners for their unconditional love and support.

Introduction

I have worked as a counsellor for individuals, couples and families affected by Asperger syndrome (AS) for over 13 years. In that time I have encountered many different people from a variety of backgrounds and cultures, some of whom left a lasting impression upon me. One such couple had travelled from Ireland to see me, with the purpose of trying to sort out their 45-year marriage, which had become a collection of long-term misunderstandings and misinterpretations.

During the course of counselling it was recognised and accepted by both partners that the husband was affected by AS. They developed together a better understanding of what this meant and how AS had impacted on their relationship. They learned to appreciate the differences between them, instead of battling to change the other to become like them. The effect of this on the couple's relationship was very positive. Their relationship together and with their grown-up children improved and developed with time.

The couple found great relief in finally knowing the reason why, for years, they had both felt they were struggling to maintain the relationship. They no longer blamed each other for their problems as both now accepted the disparities between them and that it was a case, for him, of can't rather than won't! They were a fantastic couple, totally devoted to each other; two people that I would describe as 'salt of the earth'. Their love and commitment had kept them together and both wanted the best for the other. He was desperate to try to get it right and to make some sense of what he should and should not be doing but he could not figure out why, despite trying so hard, he still seemed to unintentionally get it wrong and upset her.

On a particular day, when we were working together to find strategies to improve communication, he suddenly leant forward in his chair and said to me, 'Have you got a book of rules? Is there a book out there I can read that will tell me what to do to make her happy and help me understand her?' When I told him that I did not know of one, he said, 'Well then, maybe it's time you wrote one!'

The world of relationships and women can appear to be a minefield for many men; put Asperger syndrome into the equation and it can feel like being blindfolded in a minefield! Understanding the complex nature of dating, courting and maintaining a long-term relationship requires specific skills. Men with AS can find this very difficult as they are often trying to work out their non-Asperger syndrome (non-AS) partner with logic rather than intuition. So many have discovered that there is nothing less logical than an emotional woman. Hence the accumulation of misunderstandings and unresolved issues grows within the relationship. Using logic does not work when communication is emotional and this is often why things break down and, even with the best intentions, the man will still find himself getting it wrong again and again.

Obviously every person and relationship is unique; this book does not offer all the answers or absolute solutions for anyone or everyone and the reader should take from it what applies and works for them in their particularly unique situation. Meeting a potential partner, initiating and maintaining a relationship requires a lot of work and effort; it is not an easy task regardless of whether or not someone is on the autistic spectrum. However, if one partner is on the spectrum, without doubt, the relationship is going to require more effort, motivation and work. The aspiration of this book is to provide some answers and basic rules that may make the understanding of women and relationships a little bit more comprehensible and clear.

It has taken 13 years for me to reach a point where I felt I could write this book. It is not based on scientific research; it is based upon real-life experiences. I have found myself being asked the same questions by men with AS over and over again. This book is based around those questions and I have, to the best of my knowledge and ability, both as a therapist and a woman, attempted to answer those questions. I have put into place a few rules that are easily followed. The book is divided into four parts. The first part addresses the problems and issues around the topics of dating and initiating a relationship. The second part focuses on the maintenance of relationships and areas where problems might occur. The third part considers the changes and challenges that having a child can bring to the relationship. The concluding part offers a summary of the advice given throughout the book.

The aim of the book is not just to increase an understanding of women, but also to help men with AS to understand themselves. All those years ago I was asked by my client if I could write a book of rules that would guide him to making him and his wife happy in their relationship. This book is perhaps not quite a book of rules, but a book that offers answers and hope to the man with AS in his quest for a better understanding of the puzzling world of women and relationships.

Rule 1

If she is not interested then you
must not contact her again.

Dating and Courtship

Making reference to dating and courtship can conjure up the idea that this is something that happens in youth. This, however, is not the case, and especially not the case in men with Asperger syndrome as many do not start seriously looking for a partner till they are in their thirties or forties. There are many reasons why the AS man might delay looking for a partner. Some men may have been too busy pursuing other interests to pursue dating. For others the whole prospect of trying to meet someone, date them and court them may feel so overwhelming and intimidating that although the desire is there, the thought of acting on it is far too daunting.

Sadly there is also the case where the AS man has tried to date someone and been rejected or humiliated by them; this could have knocked their confidence and may have left them feeling too scared to risk it happening again. I do try to reassure clients I see in this situation that it is worth trying again, and that it is often more about bad timing or making a poor choice of date that caused the rejection. We will then work together to find ways and strategies to avoid this happening again.

Meeting someone later in life can come with its own set of possible difficulties, as often for the women this may be a second relationship and she may already have a relationship history and children. These are things the man will have to consider before he becomes involved. Having said that, it could also be a second relationship for him, and he may also have children to consider.

Whatever their age, dating can be the one of the most difficult stages for some men with AS as it is unpredictable, involves getting to know new people, places and situations, and involves much communication. The dating stage also relies heavily on one's ability to read body language and make small talk. For these reasons the dating stage can seem very overwhelming and hard work for some men with AS, as it will require them to come out of their comfort zone.

In this first part of the book I have attempted to address the main questions and concerns I have been asked by men with AS with regards to dating. It is, however, impossible to cover all scenarios and situations; for example, the number of places a person may find love is limitless, as is the type of dates they could go on! How the date progresses will also be affected by many factors, including the couple's age, culture, religion, sexual orientation and country of origin, and it would be impossible for me to cover all possible dating scenarios. For this reason I have focused only on a selection of the most common places to meet a prospective partner and dating scenarios.

Where and how to meet someone are the questions that I am most often asked, as the desire to try to make the dating and courtship process as predictable and safe as possible is very strong in the men I encounter. Unfortunately, there is no foolproof way to meet a potential partner as there are far too many variables to take into account. It is, though, possible for the man to develop a personal strategy and to make decisions on areas that are within his control, such as how he aims to meet someone, and to have a selection of topics to discuss on the first date.

This part of the book attempts to address the areas I am asked about most often, and to offer the reader as much as I am able to prepare him for this complex and unpredictable stage in relationships. It is for the AS man to take from it what he needs and to consider the pros and cons that I have listed.

1

Where is the best place to meet a prospective partner?

The task of finding a prospective partner can seem overwhelming for the man with AS and I am often asked the best way to achieve this. To cover every possible avenue would be impossible as relationships can develop out of the most unlikely situations and encounters. I have chosen the most likely places and also the most accessible. Everyone will have a preference and what will suit one person may not suit another – it will be for the reader to decide what might work best for them. I have highlighted four of the most common areas and I have listed the pros and cons of each.

THE NIGHT CLUB SCENE

This way of meeting is rarely successful for men with AS. The majority will find night clubs distressing due to the likelihood of sensory overload, caused by the loud music, flashing lights, crowded bars and dance floors which all tend to form a large portion of the night club scene. Sensory overload can feel extremely overwhelming and some men with AS have reported finding it impossible to hold a conversation when faced with the distraction of so much background noise. This can feel quite frustrating if the man with AS wants to communicate with a woman he is trying to develop a rapport with. However, on the other side of the coin, some men with AS may find this a bonus as they can use the loud noise as an excuse to avoid small talk and long conversations. This relieves the pressure of having to think of what to say and they can just enjoy the dancing.

For the majority of men with AS, though, there is a tendency to avoid night clubs and this could also be due to a history of bad experiences. I have heard accounts of men being set up by women to make their partners jealous, or just being used to buy the drinks The difficulties caused by having Asperger syndrome coupled with an eagerness to find a girlfriend can result in some men with AS not noticing, ignoring or being unable to read the warning signs. The advice I would offer here, if the night club is an option being explored, is to go there with a group or with a friend who can be relied on for advice or to spot the warning signs. Unfortunately this is not always possible for some young men and they really can end up feeling both overwhelmed and confused by the whole experience.

Some advice

If a woman approaches a man in a club, he needs to ask himself: Why? He needs to reassure himself she is not with another man and merely trying to make that man jealous. If unsure, he should ask her if she is with her boyfriend. If she asks for a drink in the first few sentences, it would be sensible to be cautious as there is a chance she is using him purely to obtain free drinks. However, asking her if she would like a drink, offering her a compliment, or dancing within her proximity can be ways of first approaching a woman in a club. If the woman refuses the drink, ignores the compliment or moves away from his presence on the dance floor, this means she is not interested and he must not pursue it.

If he is still with the woman at the end of the evening, then he could suggest he would like to see her again or ask if she would like to exchange mobile numbers to keep in touch. If she says she would rather leave it for now then he should wish her well and make his way home. If, however, she says it would be good to see him again or agrees to him giving her a lift home, he should not presume this means she wants sex. Unless she makes it very clear by saying so and asking if he wants to have sex with her, the man should *never* presume that sex is on the agenda. Always remember that as alcohol can promote a false sense of security, it can also cause a lack of control. The man should not put himself at risk or become a risk to anyone else.

Pros

- It is more likely to offer the opportunity of a one night stand if that is what you are looking for.

- You get to dance (if you like dancing).

- It is easy to lose yourself in the crowd.

- You will not be expected to talk much.

- There will be the opportunity to meet women of different backgrounds, cultures and ages.

Cons

- It is not ideal for finding a serious or long-term partner.

- It can cause sensory overload.

- Too much alcohol can cause a false sense of security and loss of control.

- There is a risk of someone reacting violently.

- There is a risk of being used to buy drinks, cigarettes or drugs.

- It can be restricted to a younger age group.

WORK ENVIRONMENT

A large proportion of couples meet within a work environment. There is no reason why it should be any different for men with AS. It does, however, require knowledge of what the company rules are, as some places of work do not tolerate relationships within the workforce. To ignore this could result in one or both of the couple having to leave their place of employment and for many this would be both inconvenient and stressful. The consequence of this is likely to have a very negative effect on the relationship that has been recently established.

So, presuming the company does not prohibit relationships between staff, the workplace can be a way of meeting a potential partner. Obviously the type of work a person does will make a difference to this, as some jobs can be very male dominated, such as engineering or IT. If, on the other hand, the workplace offers a mixed environment and there is a woman that the man with AS is attracted to, then the workplace can offer an ideal opportunity to get to know someone. It will give both the chance to get to know each other slowly and to build up a rapport before embarking on the possibility of a relationship. This all sounds very straightforward; the difficulty I find is that some men with AS cannot tell whether a woman is actually attracted to them, or if she is merely enjoying their friendship and wants no more. I will talk more about attraction later.

Initiating a work-related relationship is sometimes left to social events such as the Christmas party, as this can achieve two things: (1) the man can see if she comes with a partner, which would rule out the possibility of taking it further, and (2) if she is alone, he can see if she seeks out his company. If the Christmas party is not an option and as long as she is not wearing a wedding or engagement ring, then the man will need to do a little detective work to discover whether she is available. This could be achieved by asking someone who knows her if she has a partner or even asking her directly.

However, this needs tact and the man with AS should tread carefully so as to avoid intruding upon her sensitivities or to make himself vulnerable to being rejected. One way forward could be to find out if any new restaurants have opened in the vicinity and then mention this and ask her whether she has been there or heard any reports about it. If she has a partner this will give her the opportunity to let the man know, by saying that she went there with her boyfriend or is planning to go with him. The majority of women will be honest and let a potential pursuer know if they are with someone, although this may not always be the case. If the man is on Facebook he could also ask her if she has a Facebook account and if so he could request to add her as a friend on Facebook – this is likely to tell him her relationship status.

If an AS man has found a woman in his workplace who he is attracted to, he will need to be quite cautious about how he approaches the possibility of a date with her. If she tells him she is with someone or ignores his attempts to strike up a conversation, then he must back off. If not he could find himself the target of ridicule or, even worse, being reported for harassment.

Having said that, work-based relationships are often successful and many of the couples I see have met this way. However, if the relationship is unsuccessful, the work environment can become a source of stress or anguish, making it very difficult for one or both to continue working there. This can be made worse if the man finds himself the target of malicious gossip. All he can do is to put on a brave face, ignore the gossip and be aware that these things soon blow over, so long as he does not react.

Pros

- There could be a common denominator between you.
- There could be time to build up a friendship first.
- There may be the ability to check out if she is in a relationship already.
- Work social events are a good time to meet someone.
- Relationships formed this way are often successful.

Cons

- Relationships may be prohibited as part of the company's policy.
- It can be difficult to determine if the woman has a partner.
- It can be difficult to be sure whether her interest is purely platonic or romantic.

- The man could become the victim of gossip if he gets it wrong or discloses too much information.

- If the relationship ends then it can make the work environment difficult.

SOCIAL OR SPECIAL INTEREST GROUPS

A search on the internet may indicate that there is a social group for single adults running in the local vicinity. Social groups are run by a section of people who work together compiling a programme of activities on different days or evenings. Members of the group then decide which events they would like to attend or take part in. For example, a programme for one week might look like this:

Programme January 2012

Mon 1st	**Walk in the hills** 6 miles. Please meet at the Dog and Trumpet car park in Weatherton (which is off the A620 Weatherton to Bridlington road) at 10.00 am for a 10.15 am start. Bring a packed lunch – we may go to the pub after the walk. Please ring Samantha if you are coming on the walk.
Tue 2nd	**Bowling** at the High Speed bowling alley in Upper Street, Bridlington. Meet upstairs in the Foyer at 7.30 pm. Cost is £3.50 for one game or £5.00 for two. Please contact John if you are going.
Wed 3rd	**Evening Walk** 4 miles. Meet at 6.30 pm to leave at 6.45 pm prompt. Drink in the Dog and Trumpet afterwards. Please contact Suki.
Thu 4th	**New Members Night.** Chance to meet new members and introduce them to the group. Meeting as usual in the Lounge Bar at 8.00 pm, White Horse Hotel, Chipwell Road, Eastly. Contact Michelle for further details.
Fri 5th	**Barn Dance** at Smithies Social Club, Upper Lane, Lowton. Lots of fun for all levels. Meet 8.00 pm. Cost £4. Contact Marvin.

Sat 6th	**Balti Night** at the Hen and Chickens, Spencer Lane, Lowton. Excellent Indian food at an affordable price. Contact Fred.
Sun 7th	**Pub night with live music** at The Brass Monkey, London Road, Spidlington. A regular venue for Rapport where you can chat with friends or dance the night away to a live band. Contact Ranjit.

The cost of joining these groups can vary and this will need to be checked out. In addition the age range of the group will also need to be checked, as some groups can be for younger adults in their twenties and thirties whereas others will be for older age groups.

Social groups can be a great way to get to know others without the pressures of having to try to initiate or form a relationship. Social groups will offer a sense of belonging and most members will be in a similar place in their lives, wanting to make friends and participate in various activities. Most will not be in a relationship and will just be looking for company and friends that they can spend time with.

Most social groups will hold a new member's night at least once a month, and it is often possible for a new member to call and let the host know that they are coming along. This could make it much easier for the individual as they can go in the knowledge that they will be greeted by someone and have someone to talk to and introduce them to the other members. Many groups offer a wide range of interests and activities to choose from, such as walking, dancing, dining, theatre and weekends away. They offer the member the choice to interact as much as they like and to come and go as they please.

As well as social groups there are also interest groups such as the Ramblers (www.ramblers.org.uk), hill-walking groups, photography groups and many others. These interest-specific groups can be ideal for a man with AS if he has a specific interest, as he will be able to share this with others as well as enjoy the social side of the group. A big bonus with meeting someone in an interest group is that they will be someone who shares the same interest and this will give both an excellent starting point in developing a relationship.

It is important to remember that when an individual with AS is in a group situation their brain will be working extra hard to keep up to speed and react to the social cues around them. There may be a need to limit the time spent interacting in the group or it may be worth taking a little break by popping outside or finding a quiet place for a few minutes.

Pros

- Prior arrangement will mean there is someone to meet you.
- There is no pressure to have a relationship.
- You will be able to get to know someone first.
- There are lots of different venues and activities.
- You can find someone who shares your interests.

Cons

- You might not get on with everyone in the group.
- Some groups are expensive to join or charge to join in the activities.
- Being part of a group could be hard work and quite tiring for you.

DATING SITES

Internet dating for many men with AS may seem to be an ideal choice as it gives the chance to actually choose a woman in advance that they find attractive from her photograph and who appears to share their interests. It will mean that the initial contact will be via email, which for many of the men I have worked with felt far less threatening than having a one to one conversation.

Being able to arrange the first meeting is another major bonus in using dating sites and I have known some men go to great lengths to try to get this right. For example, one man with AS made a trip out to the restaurant where he had arranged to meet his date the following night. He found a good place to park his car and checked what change he might need for the parking meter, and he timed how long it took him to get there by car and then by foot to the restaurant.

He chose a place for them to sit in and chose which seating position he preferred for himself, which in this case was to have his back against the wall. He studied the menu, decided what he would eat and how much it would cost, made a note of where the toilets were and asked about the wines. By doing this he reduced the fear factor he suffered from of encountering unpredictable problems on the night. When he went on to have his date, he was more relaxed and felt more confident than he would have been without the planning. I am happy to say that they went on to a second date.

Internet dating can allow the man with AS to feel more in control than he would in a random situation; however, it is important that it does not become a way of life and a habit. Internet dating for some men with AS can become an obsession which can actually be the downfall of a relationship that could have worked. Before internet dating, the prospect of ending a relationship and finding someone new could feel quite daunting and, to avoid this, a couple would often choose to work harder to maintain what they had and work to improve their relationship together. Internet dating could be called 'people shopping' and it can become just that. A quest to find the best! Hence as soon as the initial passionate stage in a relationship is over and an extra effort is needed to make the relationship exciting and intimate, it can be easier to shop around for someone new with no shared history, rather than to work at the present relationship.

In some men with AS their ability to read other people's motives and hidden agendas is extremely limited. This will often make them unable to tell whether someone is being deceitful or friendly. This difficulty in reading others' motives can make them vulnerable to exploitation when dating, especially to financial exploitation. If the man earns a good salary, this can make him a prime target for being taken advantage of financially. If a man with AS finds himself continuously out of pocket in a relationship, then he needs to pull back from being overgenerous and see what reaction this causes from the woman. If a woman is genuine then she will understand and a compromise and agreement will be made. On the other hand, if a man is in a financial position that allows him to pay for everything and he is happy to do this, then that is entirely up to him.

I have also encountered clients who have talked of meeting women on international dating sites from foreign countries who were very keen for marriage. It has later transpired that the women's main motive for the relationship was to gain access to a new country of residence. Although this is likely to be a rare occurrence it is a possibility worth noting. Obviously there is no way he can be totally sure if her motives are genuine until they are together as a couple but it might help if he visits her in her own environment or if he introduces her to his friends and family to seek their opinion.

The main problem that seems to occur for men with AS is that an addiction to internet dating may develop. This may be caused by the man with AS having low self-esteem and holding on to the belief that the cure for his difficulties lies in finding the 'right' woman. For example, a couple might meet this way and in the beginning she will be his obsession, the focus of his attention and thoughts. However, after a while, when the relationship becomes more down to earth and the passion subsides, he may feel disappointed and then decide that she is not right for him, that she deceived him into thinking she was. He could then decide that he has still not found the right woman and start the search all over again. I have known this pattern to continue for many years for some men until eventually their resources run out.

Pros

- There is the chance to select someone who seems suitable.

- There is access to women from other cultures or countries.

- There is the chance to build a rapport using email rather than having to make conversation.

- It is possible to have built a rapport by the first meeting.

- A place and time for meeting can be selected.

- It allows the option of checking the venue beforehand.

Cons

- You may not always get replies to your emails.

- Emails may not lead to a date.

- A date may not turn up.

- The person you meet may not look the same as their photograph.

- You could be set up for financial gain or other rewards.

- Until you meet the person you will not know if there is any chemistry between you.

- Internet dating can become an obsession.

Rule 2

Never assume that her feelings
are the same as yours and
the attraction is mutual.

2

How do I know if she is attracted to me?

If it is a first encounter and a woman is attracted to a man, she will look into his eyes and she will also smile – just a fleeting smile – and then she will look away. As long as he smiles back she will look again and smile. If they are already in communication the man may notice that she leans her body towards him and maybe makes physical contact with him in conversation. For example, she could affectionately touch his arm while talking. What do these simple gestures signal for a man with AS?

The world of dating and all the complexities it brings can feel like a nightmare for men with AS, as it involves being able to read the other person's body language, facial expressions and voice intonation. These are all things men with AS will find very difficult to do. A woman may be quite careful in avoiding appearing over-keen in the early stages of meeting as, like a man with AS, she may fear rejection. Putting together his difficulty in mindreading and her reluctance to show that she is attracted to him will make it almost impossible for the man with AS to figure out whether a woman likes him romantically or just as a friend.

In clinical trials on mindreading, AS men were found to do less well than non-AS men (Baron-Cohen et al. 2001). A typical three- to four-year-old would be able to demonstrate the ability to apply theory of mind, whereas in children affected by Asperger syndrome theory of mind does not begin to develop till between the ages of 9 and 14 (Happe and Frith 1995). Theory of mind is the brain mechanism that is responsible for empathy (not sympathy – these are quite different) and reading the more subtle non-verbal signals that are given out in communication. Asperger syndrome will cause a difficulty in mindreading and being able to empathise with others; this has been found at all developmental levels throughout the life span (Ozonoff, Roger and Pennington 1991).

Difficulty in reading the social cues given out by others will cause a problem for a man with AS in getting the timing right in the dating game, as it will not come naturally for him. This can be made even more difficult by the probability that there may already be a history of him being rejected by his peers and a learned knowledge that he can sometimes misread other people. This alone could greatly undermine his confidence in knowing whether he is getting the pacing right.

The man will now be in the situation that he has found a woman he likes and is attracted to. However, he is now left without any idea of whether his feelings and desires are reciprocated; furthermore, if they are, whether that is on a romantic or friendship level. Obviously if the woman has clearly vocalised her feelings then this will not be a problem, but this is highly unlikely, as she may also fear rejection or the risk of being accused of being too forward.

Figuring out whether or not the attraction is reciprocated can put some men with AS through absolute torment, sometimes affecting both their health and state of mind. This is one area that relies almost totally on body language and the signals that are given out and received. For the man with AS, looking at another person's face for subtle clues is about as useful as looking at a blank canvas, in that it gives them no information or even clues as to what the other person is feeling.

Sometimes problems can arise from the man with AS making the assumption that if he likes a woman then she must feel the same about him and the attraction is mutual. This is often not the case and it is important that this is never assumed unless the woman has absolutely spelled out her feelings of attraction to him. The reason this misassumption can occur is lack of theory of mind, and not being able to see the situation from the other person's viewpoint. The only mindset the man with AS will be aware of will be his own feelings, and these feelings of attraction may be very strong. The strength of his feelings may be exaggerated due to his eagerness to find a girlfriend and it is this that may cause him to presume that the woman shares his attraction and feels as strongly as he does.

This misreading can also happen in reverse and I find some clients can hold the belief that others are thinking negatively about them, just by catching sight of another person's glance or a look. They will miss the fact that a woman is flirting with them or finds them attractive. In either case the assumption could be wrong and this is why it is crucial to check out just what the woman is feeling before any action is taken. It is important not to get too carried away by feelings of attraction to a particular woman or to assume she feels the same, as it might appear that you are being too forward. The woman may regard the man with AS as being egotistical or arrogant and his chances of wooing her will be lost.

Attraction is shown in body language and often it is the timing of the look or smile which signals to another that the attraction is there. When a woman is giving signals that she is attracted to a man, she will maintain eye contact a few seconds longer than would normally occur. Unfortunately it will be almost impossible for the man with AS to gauge this. Eye contact can be difficult for some men with AS to make, and they will struggle with making or maintaining eye contact, especially when in communication.

One of the reasons for this is that they may find it very difficult to concentrate on what they or the other is saying if they are trying to maintain eye contact or read another person's eye contact. Reading eye contact skills do vary amongst the men I see and some are more adept at this than others. I have found some will go to great lengths to try to improve this skill by attending neuro-linguistic programming (NLP) courses, reading body language books or simply from observation of films and soaps.

If a woman's look could be filmed and the man with AS had long enough to study and analyse the glance and time it, he would probably figure out what she meant. Unfortunately, though, this look is over in seconds, so if the man with AS does have a feeling or a sense that a woman's eye contact is flirtatious then he needs to check that the rest of her face, and her body and voice are also indicating she is attracted to him.

It was found that two-year-old autistic toddlers were inclined to give more attention to looking at the mouth rather than the eyes in comparison to non-autistic toddlers (Jones, Carr and Klin 2008). It is likely the man with AS will unconsciously be doing the same, and will be reading a person's mouth expressions rather than their eyes. For men with AS, it can feel far safer to be governed by the mouth or how close a woman places herself next to him than trying to rely on the eyes. This can make a man with AS quite vulnerable, as it means he will not be able to tell when he is being deceived, as good deceivers always smile.

I have listed some of the signs to look for that might demonstrate that a woman is interested, or not, as the case may be.

EYES
Possibly interested

- She makes longer than normal eye contact.
- She looks away and looks back quite quickly.

Not interested

- She may look away.
- She may look down but give brief darting glances.

MOUTH
Possibly interested

- She smiles; this can be quite slight.
- She pouts.

Not interested

- She does not smile at all.

- She will only smile at you in a greeting or if you say something funny.

- She will give a very tight-lipped smile which may suggest she is nervous or annoyed.

PROXIMITY
Possibly interested

- If sitting by you or in front of you she will lean towards you.

- She will allow you to come into her space or she will come into yours and stand or sit quite close to you.

- Her arms will be open and welcoming.

Not interested

- She will lean away from you.

- She will make sure that there is no physical touch between you.

- She will keep her arms folded.

TOUCH
Possibly interested

- She may make physical contact with you; this could be a pat, rubbing your arm, allowing her foot or knee to make contact with you.

- She may give a hug when saying goodbye or greeting you.

Not interested

- She will pull away from any physical contact.

- Her greetings and goodbyes will be brief and short with no attempt to touch you.

BODY MOVEMENTS
Possibly interested

- She may keep playing with her hair or pushing it back.
- Her arms are open.
- Her feet are pointed towards you.
- She maintains eye contact.

Not interested

- Her arms are folded.
- She looks away.
- She gazes past you.
- She points her feet away from you.

COMMUNICATION
Possibly interested

- She asks questions.
- She gives compliments.
- She laughs with you (not at you).

Not interested

- She gives short one-syllable answers.
- She sighs.
- She doesn't ask you questions.

This list is not foolproof, as it cannot take into account a woman's personality; she may be very shy and therefore feel nervous and display a closed body language. On the other hand, some women are very tactile and demonstrative and although they will appear very friendly they will not be flirting at all. It must also be taken into account whether a woman has been drinking alcohol, as this will lessen her inhibitions, making her more likely to show affectionate or flirty behaviour indiscriminately. If the man with AS is able to ask someone else's opinion this would be helpful. If this is not possible then he might consider telling her in a text that he really likes her and will soon discover by her reply if his feelings are reciprocated. If the woman feels the same then that will be great; if she does not, he must respect this and not attempt to take it any further.

She is unlikely to be offended by knowing he likes her, however, if he pursues her and does not respect her feelings she will be offended and he will run the risk of being accused of harassment.

3

How do I ask her out?

This needs to be done with care and caution as the man with AS needs to protect himself from feeling rejected in the event that her answer is no. Of course it is impossible to avoid the possibility that she will say no and there are many reasons why she may do this, such as the fact she is already involved with someone or that she simply does not want a relationship with anyone at the moment. Her reasons could be nothing to do with the man with AS on a personal level at all; however, it is very difficult not to feel hurt and rejected by a negative response.

There are some measures that can be taken to avoid being rebuffed and whether or not these can be applied will depend upon the circumstances and context in which the couple have met. I have chosen the three likeliest situations and will address each one accordingly.

WORK ENVIRONMENT

Forming relationships in the workplace needs to be approached with care and caution and it is understandable where the saying 'don't mix work with pleasure' comes from. Having said that, I encounter many couples who have met through their work and found that their relationship has worked very well, due to the fact they shared a strong common denominator, their work. This connection between them has in many cases given them the bonus of a shared interest, providing much to discuss and share views on.

Knowing when and how to ask a work colleague out is easier than it might first appear, as it can be achieved in a very non-committal way. For example, work situations offer an abundance of opportunities to make the offer of going for a coffee or a sandwich at lunchtime or having a quick drink after work. Making these suggestions would not be deemed as inappropriate, as long as they are approached in a light-hearted friendly manner. Sharing a coffee break or lunch will give the opportunity to get to know each other better and discover if any more interests are shared. If things seem to be going well, it could be taken further by the suggestion of meeting up outside work, for a drink or a meal.

If, though, at any stage in the process of getting to know her, whether it is asking about sharing a coffee or going out after work, she declines the offer or finds an excuse not to join him, then the man will need to say that that is fine and move the conversation on to another topic, such as a work issue. He must resist the urge to ask why or ask her out again, as the consequence could be that she will feel he is harassing her.

A SOCIAL EVENT OR INTEREST GROUP

Having a shared interest works well in AS/non-AS relationships and is a great way for couples to meet. For some couples it has been dancing lessons or a walking group or one of the many other group activities available. Meeting this way allows time to build up a rapport and gain knowledge of each other; a couple can take time to become friends before taking things further.

To take things further would mean agreeing to meet outside the social environment and this can be approached quite honestly by acknowledging the compatibility of interests they share and how it would be great to get to know each other better and see how it goes. She can either say yes or no and as long as he respects her decision and does not harass her or become resentful of her, they will both be able to continue as friends within the group and he will be free to seek a different partner if he wishes.

DATING SITES

If the man with AS met his partner on a dating site then asking her out can be less complex and more straightforward, as meeting up should be the eventual aim for both of them once a positive connection has been made. There are, though, still guidelines that should avoid getting it wrong or being rejected by her.

Before arranging an initial meeting it might be wise to talk on the phone, as this will help determine if there is a rapport between them. I have worked with some men with AS who find some voice tones or accents particularly irritating, and if this was the case then it would be pointless to pursue a relationship with the person. However, having said this, for some men with AS talking on the telephone is not always an easy option and I have worked with some men who have a real fear of using the phone and find it difficult to sound confident and articulate.

There is no easy way around this and the only way forward might be for the man to be honest and write or text. He could say he is concerned that he might not come across very well on the phone and would rather just meet up, if that is OK with her. The lady in question can then either say yes or no to this. If the answer is no then he may well have to make the effort to call her or just leave it there and look for someone else.

If he does feel confident to chat on the phone then he might want to explore this route and see how he feels after they have spoken. He might ask himself whether he found her easy to talk to. Did they find much to converse about? Did she ask to talk to him again? If the answers are yes then arrange to call again. If she agrees then it is sometimes best to send a text before calling to ask if she is free to talk, and if not when the best time to call would be. If she does not reply then he would be best to leave it there in case she is having second thoughts. It will be hard to deny the urge to call her again but if she wants to make contact she will, and is more likely to so if she does not feel pressurised into doing so.

For some men with AS being able to arrange to talk beforehand will allow them time to plan what they are going to talk about and take some of the unpredictability out of the equation. Communication is like playing a game of tennis, and each person needs to remember to bat the ball back into the other person's court, otherwise the communication, like a game of tennis, will grind to a halt. One way to keep up the communicative flow is to always finish a sentence with a question; this will help to keep the conversation going.

It might help the man to make a list beforehand of what he wants to know about her; this might be her occupation, whether she has children, how old they are, what her hobbies and interests are, and how long she has been alone for. Having this list to hand when he calls can act as a valuable prompt. It is important that he does not go into a monologue at any time about himself or his special interests. He will need to show an interest in her and offer information about himself when asked or when it is related to the topics that are being discussed.

How to end a conversation can be difficult for him, and the best way is to try to end on a positive note, maybe by saying that it was lovely to talk to her and that it would be great to meet up when she is ready. If, though, she says nothing and ignores this statement then it would be best if he did not ask her again; the suggestion has been made and for now there is little more he can do to take things further. Women sometimes like to think things over and may even want to ask a friend's opinion before they give an answer; this is OK and shows she is taking things seriously. It is important that the man does not become pushy or appear too eager, as this could scare her away. The woman will let him know when she is ready to take it further. However, her silence could mean that she has decided that she does not want to take it any further and he will have to respect this. Once again he will need to leave it there and not pressurise her any further.

4

Where do I take her on the first date and what can I do to make a good first impression?

That first date is special and is something that many women will ruminate upon and contemplate as many take much pleasure from this time of being wooed and receiving romantic attention. This is probably why a man might feel under pressure to get it right. Trying to get it right can be a struggle for some AS men, especially trying to think of somewhere special to take her or what to arrange. Most will suggest a meal, which can work quite well as it gives a focus beyond the meeting – that is, food. The food can provide a topic of conversation, especially if the woman enjoys cooking, baking or eating out. However, going out for a meal does involve quite lengthy conversations and some AS men may struggle with this and might prefer just to meet for a quick drink or coffee.

If keeping a conversation going is difficult or a concern then a good alternative may be to go to the cinema, theatre or opera, or to listen to a band or orchestra as this will limit the communication and give a common interest to discuss in the interval or when the show has finished. If the couple have met at work or in a social group and already have a friendship then they might arrange to eat together on the same evening.

If, though, the couple have met through a dating site and have not seen each other before it might be better to keep the meeting brief as a precautionary measure in the event of it not feeling right or finding the person is not what was expected. If this is the case maybe meeting for a couple of drinks or a coffee would be safer and allow the opportunity to make a hasty retreat.

It is important that the man makes the effort to present himself as well as he can. So a quick word here about personal hygiene. An absolute turn off for women is a man who is obviously unwashed, unshaven, unkempt or shabbily dressed. Besides the fact that he will not look aesthetically appealing, it could be an indication to her of how much he values her opinion and whether he considers her to be worth the effort of having a wash, brushing his teeth, shaving or trimming his beard or moustache, dressing in presentable clean clothes and cleaning his shoes.

If a man turns up on a date looking unkempt, with bad breath or body odour, it is unlikely he will see her for a second date if this is the best he can do to impress her. So giving time and consideration to appearances and hygiene is important. It is also a good idea not to eat anything beforehand that is going to repeat and result in the woman being showered with offensive burps. Bad breath is a major turn off for most people, and women do appear to revel in nice smells, so if a man uses aftershave or deodorant it can go a long way.

Whatever the couple decide to do on the first date, it is important for the AS man to remember that most women do enjoy a bit of romance. It can be the simple things the man does that will give the woman a good and lasting impression of their date and will go far in making her feel both feminine and special. The AS man could make an effort to open the door for the woman, bring her some flowers, compliment her appearance; he could be the one to go to the bar for drinks or simply walk on the outside of the pavement. At the end of the evening he could offer to walk her to her car, bus stop or home. If she is making her own way home text to ensure she arrived home safely. This will all be noted and remembered by her. These little gestures can make so much difference to how the woman will feel, both about herself and her date.

Rule 3

Do not spend the first date talking about your special interests.

5

What should I talk about on the first date?

What to talk about on the first date is often a major concern for many men with AS. It can be the cause of much stress and lengthy agonising over what they are going to converse about; especially the whole concern of having to use small talk. Small talk and Asperger syndrome do not go well together and for someone with AS initiating and maintaining irrelevant social chit chat is almost impossible. It requires a lot of thought and hard work on their part.

One of the fears about small talk is that it can feel irrelevant and unpredictable, which is why it can help to have a script stored away in memory to apply in case of emergencies. One useful strategy can be to have maybe five or six reliable and trusted questions or statements that can be called upon when a silence prevails in the conversation. To be able to put these questions together, though, does require knowing just what a woman might want the man to ask. Of course every woman and situation will be different and every woman will have different interests. The majority, though, will want to feel that the man is interested in them and is pleased with her appearance. They will expect him to be able to make them feel good, and an excellent way to begin is by offering a compliment about how she looks. The man might compliment her hair, her smile, her perfume or what she is wearing. So to have a couple of rehearsed compliments can be useful and certainly help break the ice when you first meet. Be careful about making comments that are too personal or sexual at this early stage in courtship as this could be interpreted as a sexual come on, which for some will feel too forward or threatening. For example, making a comment that she has generous boobs or a voluptuous bottom is unlikely to be well received at this stage.

As we saw earlier, communication is like playing tennis or badminton; both involve hitting the ball back into the other person's court. An excellent way of doing this and maintaining the flow of communication is to always end a sentence with a question. For example, let us first look at what happens if questions are not asked and short replies, without any elaboration, are all that is offered: the conversation will soon dry up and dissolve. This is shown in the following example of a conversation between John and Mary, who have just met on their first date. They have made their greetings and sat down to share a coffee:

Mary 'I am pleased we have met up at last. I was not sure I was going to make it tonight as my mother called to say she was not feeling very well. She has been on her own since my father died. Do you still have both your parents, John?'

John 'No, both have passed away.'

Mary 'Oh sorry, that must have been hard for you. How long ago did you lose them?'

John 'My father died in 1999 and my mother in 2001.'

Mary 'You lost them both close together then. That must have been really difficult. Did you have some support at the time?'

John 'No.'

Mary 'Oh dear, that must have been a bad time for you?'

John [not knowing what to say] 'Mmmmm.'

Mary [now finding this really hard work and trying to change the conversation] 'It is not very warm in here. The weather has been so cold lately; did you get caught in the rain on the way here?'

John 'Yes.'

Mary is now deciding she is not enjoying herself and wondering how soon she can escape the situation and go home. She does not see John for a second date.

Now let us look at how the conversation might have gone if John had remembered, as in a game of tennis, to hit the ball back into Mary's court by always ending his statements with a question.

Mary 'I am pleased we have met up at last. I was not sure I was going to make it tonight as my mother called to say she was not feeling very well. She has been on her own since my father died. Do you still have both your parents, John?'

John 'No, both have passed away. How long ago did your father pass away?'

Mary 'It was ten years ago, quite unexpected; he died of lung cancer and yet he never smoked. How long ago did you lose your parents?'

John 'My father died in 1999 and my mother in 2001; both were affected by a long-term illness so it was not unexpected. You said your mother was unwell; is she all right now, do you want to call her?'

Mary 'That is nice of you, John, I am worried about her so I think I would like to call in a little while, but let's carry on our chat. I find you really easy to talk to. Tell me about your work? You said you design web sites? I would love to know more about it.'

John is now on safe ground. He remembers not to go into too much detail and to end by asking her about her work, and yes, they do meet for a second date.

In the example above John illustrated in a few sentences that: (1) he had listened to what she said, and (2) he had considered how it made her feel. Knowing that he is able to listen to her thoughts and opinions and show he can understand how she feels are two indicators to a woman that the man is caring, considerate and thoughtful. If the woman enquires as to whether he has had a good day at work and he replies with a simple yes, then the ball will be staying in his side of the court. If, however, he replies with, 'Yes, I had quite a good day, how has your day been?'

she can then reply to his question and will be likely to end by responding with another question.

Reciprocal communication works by asking questions, and it will help if he has a memorised list of topics he can ask her questions about. Areas that should be quite safe to enquire about could be questions about her, her work, her interests, her views and beliefs, her family and her children (if she has any). She may also be asking him questions and it will be important for him to make the effort not to start talking in too much detail about his interests and dominating the communication.

Being able to read the non-verbal signals that are being transmitted during communication can give the signal for when it is time to change topic or bring the conversation to an end. These signals may not always be very obvious to a man affected by AS, so it is important for him to be aware that he may not always pick up the 'I am bored' signals on her face. For example, one gentleman on a first date managed to manoeuvre the conversation onto the topic of motorbikes, which was his special interest; the woman soon became knowledgeable about every bike he had owned, including the registration numbers.

At the end of the evening he told her he thought she was quieter than he had expected. He was quite taken aback when she exasperatedly informed him that she would not have been so quiet if he had allowed her to get a word in or he had thought to ask her a question about herself. She did not see him for a second date.

The lesson here is for him not to allow himself to get embroiled in talking about his special interest (unless they both share the same interest) and to have a memorised checklist to fall back on to keep the communication between them flowing more smoothly. It is worth remembering that the majority of people like to talk about themselves and their interests, so have a few prearranged questions based on the knowledge you have already gained about her.

For some men with AS, eye contact can be difficult and trying to converse while trying to maintain appropriate eye contact can affect their ability to concentrate, formulate their words and listen to what is being said. If this is the case then it is worth the AS man taking the time to consider carefully where he stands or sits in relation to her. If it is possible he should avoid sitting or standing opposite his date as this will bring her attention to his eye contact. If he places himself slightly to her side then eye contact will be obscured and as long as he remembers to nod or shake his head in response to her comments then she will not be confused by his lack of or evasive eye contact.

Other rules the AS man might follow could be not to interrupt the woman when she is talking and not to overgeneralise his thoughts and opinions onto the rest of the male population. An example of this would be to say that he preferred women with blonde hair, just like every other man on the planet. This could be read as a complete overgeneralisation and very narrow minded, and would not be very well received.

There is a general rule of topics to avoid at this early stage in the courtship, unless of course it is already known that both people share the same opinion as each other. These are:

- politics
- religion
- morality
- sex
- how to discipline children
- women drivers
- her weight, appearance or dress sense (unless complimentary)
- the Third World
- capital punishment
- mental health
- physical health

- his special interest (unless it is shared or she expresses an interest in it)
- his ex (if he has one)
- anything that makes him angry, upset or regretful.

At the end of the evening it is worthwhile always to try to finish on a positive note, which can easily be achieved by him saying how much he has enjoyed the evening, the company and the conversation. If the AS man has decided he would like to see the woman again, then he can say so. However, it is best not to expect that the woman will want to arrange it with him there and then. It is simply a way of letting her know he is happy to see her again, but is willing to let her contact him when she is free. This way she will not feel under pressure and will appreciate him giving her time to consider. She may well want to arrange another date there and then, which will feel great; however, if she does not do this and neither does she make contact then the man must leave it there and not harass her with texts and calls.

6

How do I know when or if to take it further?

In my research (Aston 2001, p.28) I asked non-AS females to describe what attracted them to their AS partners, and the information that came back basically shared the same thread throughout. Many stated that they felt the man they met was a complete gentleman; they described him as gentle, kind, quiet, well mannered, attentive and having other positive qualities, all of which they identified very early on in their first meetings. For many this was very different from the sexually focused men they had encountered in the past.

The women were very taken by the AS man and appreciated that he did not put pressure on them to be physically intimate. However, some did find that after a few dates they began to question whether he actually fancied them as he had not made any advances towards them. They were becoming unsure as to whether the AS man was perhaps looking for a platonic relationship.

The women were totally unaware that the AS man was probably struggling with being able to tell what they wanted from him and whether it was indeed safe to take the relationship further. He was unable to read from their mannerisms or body language whether it was OK to hold their hand, put his arm around them or kiss. Trying to work this out can be a nightmare for him and he may agonise endlessly over whether it is safe for him to take the relationship into another dimension. How to tell what to do is certainly one of the questions I am often asked, as the AS man tries to figure out what the woman really wants from him and whether she actually fancies him.

Once again the signs a woman gives off that she is attracted to a man can be very subtle and not easy to read; the reason for this is that the woman does not want to get it wrong either. She does not want the AS man to feel she is too forward or end up being rejected by him. Many women still hold on to the notion that it is for the man to initiate or to make the first move and will often also hold the belief that he will have read her non-verbal signals that it is OK to make a move, such as hold her hand or kiss her.

So how can an AS man find out what she wants? One way to check out if she wants more than a platonic relationship with him is for him to touch her in a way that is friendly and not sexual and see how she responds. For example, if they have gone out for a meal and her hands are on the table he might try resting his hand by hers and see if she moves her hand closer or if she quickly pulls her hand away. If she does not pull away then the man might gently take her hand and hold it in his. Likewise, when they are walking together the man might offer his arm to link or ask if he may hold her hand. Asking permission is always the safest way, but for some AS men their fear of rejection is so strong that they find they cannot ask the question. What if the woman says no? If this is the case it might feel safer to use texting or emailing to ask if she would like more from the relationship or not.

Texting or emailing has been a life saver for some men and using this form of communication has felt much safer for them. An ideal time to text is often after a date, saying something like: 'Hello Mary. You looked absolutely lovely tonight; it was very hard for me not to kiss you! Love John x'

Once this is sent he will need to wait to see what she sends back. The woman may text saying she is not ready for that or does not feel that way. If she does then it is good that he has found out before he did try to take it further and found himself in a very uncomfortable and difficult situation. Or she just may say: 'Thank you John. Yes I wish you had kissed me! Love Mary x'

If it is the latter then he has his answer and next time the couple meet up he may wish to try a gentle kiss at the end of the date.

You may have noticed I used the wording 'gentle kiss'. How a person kisses is very important for the majority of women and also often seen as indicating what kind of lover the man will be. The first kiss is something that the woman will remember and replay in her mind. This is a very important move and it is another part of courtship that the man needs to try to get right; it can almost be seen as the crossroads that will take the dating into an intimate relationship or end it dead in its tracks.

Kissing should be romantic and respectful; it should be soft, gentle and focused. When a person is attracted to another or sexually aroused the lips become very sensitive to touch. For some women there is nothing worse than being kissed in a way that could leave them feeling as though their mouths have been forcefully raped! There is nothing worse than being kissed by someone who is invasive with their tongue or covers the woman's mouth with their saliva. These are major turn offs and will signal to the woman that if this is how the man kisses then this is how he will treat her in bed.

Another rule is for the AS man not to interpret a kiss as a free licence to start touching the woman's breasts, bottom or vagina. The man may stroke the non-erogenous areas of her body such as her back, arms or her hair but that should be as far as he takes it at this stage, unless she makes it very obvious by giving a clear physical or verbal indication that she would like more from him, for example, if she touches the man's penis or verbally asks him to touch her. Even then it would still be worth him checking it out by asking her the question.

After the kiss it would make her feel good if he gave her a compliment, such as telling her he has wanted to kiss her since he first met her or that she is gorgeous. It is the small things he does that she will remember at this stage. For him to show her respect while letting her know he finds her a very desirable woman will all be part of the journey into the next stage, the sexual stage.

7

When is it OK to expect sex?

The sex angle of dating is a minefield for the AS man and the most important thing he will need to know and always remember is that he must never presume that because a woman is friendly or affectionate it means she will have sex with him.

There have been cases when young AS men have been set up by their friends and been given information that was not true and believed it, and this has led them into trouble. For example, a young man in his early twenties was told by his mates that if a woman allowed a guy to walk her home this meant she would be willing to have sex with him when he got her home. The young man I saw on bail had been charged with attempted rape because he had believed what his friends had told him. When a young girl agreed to let him walk her home, he had overstepped the mark and lost control of his sexual desires and ignored her resistance, believing so strongly that she really wanted him. Only the fact that someone saw and intervened prevented it from being much worse.

So how is it possible for a man to know what a woman wants, unless she has explicitly spelled it out for him by saying she wants to have sex with him? The answer to this is simple – no man can ever be sure, and the safest way is never to make that assumption that she does or try to cross her boundaries unless she has said it is OK and is also initiating sex with him. I am going to give another word of warning here: if she is intoxicated with alcohol or has taken drugs then whatever she says the man would be wise not to have sexual intercourse with her, because she may regret it when she sobers up and accuse him of taking advantage of her. If they have spent the night together and in the morning she states she wants to make love with him then he has her sober-minded consent, so he can go ahead and enjoy!

Although the AS man will have difficulty reading the more subtle non-verbal cues a woman might give he is more than capable of reading the very obvious cues. If they are spending an evening together in one or the other's home and have been caressing and kissing and then she starts to undress him, touch him sexually or places his hand on her breasts or vagina then he may feel it is safe to reciprocate. If she obviously encourages him to continue and he has an erection and by touching her vagina discovers she is quite wet and excited by him then he can ask her if she would like to make love with him. If she says yes and is still welcoming, then continue and enjoy. If she says no or that she is not sure, then do not attempt intercourse but continue with the petting and stimulating each other by mutual masturbation.

If a man remembers never to put the woman under pressure and to offer her respect then she will respect him and the relationship will have a much higher chance of developing into something very worthwhile and long lasting.

8

What if she rejects me? How can I avoid this happening?

Finding a person whom one is attracted to, is compatible with, shares the same interests and is intellectually matched can feel really difficult to achieve. However, being able to tell whether or not his feelings are reciprocated can be difficult for men with AS.

Men with AS may already have a history of feeling rejected and the fear is often that this could happen again in the future and will be almost impossible to avoid. Sometimes the rejection comes at the first move, such as if the woman is asked for a dance; other times it might be after the first date. If this happens then it is almost impossible for the one rejected not to feel hurt, resentful and sometimes as though he is a total failure. AS men can take rejection very personally, though sometimes it will have nothing to do with them at all and may be about something which is totally out of their control. There can be many reasons why his advances have been rejected, and often it is about the wrong timing or the woman's situation at the time.

Sometimes I have found that AS men might aim too high in their expectations and desires and find themselves pursuing the most attractive and intelligent women they can find, who, to be honest, in some cases are way out of their league. I recommend to clients that they give themselves a rating out of 10 for attractiveness; let's assume that the rating was 7 out of 10. Then using pictures or magazines I ask them to rate pictures of women out of 10. Then I look to see how the ratings compare in relation to themselves and the woman they find attractive and often they are totally unrealistic.

For example, they might rate themselves at 6 or 7, but then I discover the women they want to meet could be rated at 9 or 10.

The rule in attraction is that you always need to stay at the same rating as yourself and try not to go up or down more than one level. This information is very useful if the man is exploring dating sites or considering someone he has met at work or in an interest group. So if a man rates himself at 7 he should be looking for a prospective partner who would be rated at between 6 and 8. If the man is rating himself alone then he might ask a trusted friend or family member, and maybe the women he knows, to rate him to check out if their perspective is the same as his. The aim is that when looking for a prospective partner, both are in a similar league and complement each other. If not, rejection could follow.

Unfortunately, even when the attraction level is matched things can still go wrong and there may be many other reasons why his feelings for her are not reciprocated. For some women a man's financial bracket or job title is more important than how he looks. Studies have supported the fact that whereas men will often look for youth and attractiveness, women will look for wealth and security. If this is the case it would not matter how the man presented himself – if he is neither wealthy nor in a high employment position then he may find himself rejected. He will need to console himself with the knowledge that it is her loss and she is unlikely to be the type of woman he would have been compatible with. This, though, is not the case for all women and there are many women who do not have money as their top priority and will accept a man for who he is rather than what he earns or possesses.

Finally, it may be just about the timing, and it cannot be presumed that just because a woman is on her own she is looking to be in a relationship. She may be still getting over an ex-boyfriend, she may be gay and not interested sexually in males, she may just like being independent or on her own. So if the woman's answer is no, the man will have to accept her choice and move on; he must not try to convince her otherwise and must avoid showing resentment or cynicism; this will only cause friction and leave a bad taste in the long run. Just because a woman says no to a relationship, that does not mean she will not want to remain friends or, in some cases, give it time and see what develops in the future.

The Relationship

From the moment a mutual attraction between a couple has been established, the dynamics of that relationship start to change and it begins to take on a new and more relaxed perspective. This stage is the courtship stage and can feel more comfortable than the previous dating stage, which is usually a time of unpredictability and uncertainty. The courtship stage begins when the couple make the conscious decision, either through verbal or, more usually, intimate expression, that they want to be more than friends, that their feelings are deeper than mere friendship and that there is a mutual (physical) attraction. Although this attraction will have a physical basis, it will also have an intellectual, psychological and, in many cases, spiritual base.

This courtship stage will be a time for the couple to become more familiar with one another's ways, interests, beliefs, opinions, families, history, sexuality, spirituality and personality. They are then drawn, quite naturally, into the passionate, or honeymoon, stage, which is about getting to know someone on a deeper level. This is invariably a very exciting and stimulating time in the development of the relationship and is a crucial foundation stone that needs to be laid down for the relationship to be further built upon.

Many women I have spoken with, within my professional capacity, really do relate to this passionate stage and often describe it as being the happiest time that they have shared with their partner; they talk about his attraction to her, his attentiveness, his eagerness to please her and desire to be with her. The women have described this time as a time of being made to feel special, relevant and truly appreciated by him. Sadly, many women go on to describe how quickly this stage seems to come to an end; for some women it feels as if, quite literally, overnight, he loses interest and all that romantic attention suddenly, lamentably and, in the woman's mind, prematurely comes to an end. The women mourn this time and long to have it back again. The end of this passionate stage normally coincides with the couple making a decision to start living together and/or marry, which then leads the couple to move from the passionate stage to the compassionate stage or, as I see it, a very pragmatic stage.

Relationships, if they are to have a chance of survival and growth, need to progress from the passionate to the compassionate stage, and this will normally happen after about the first six months. In unhealthy relationships which are affected by issues such as abuse or infidelity, it is unlikely that trust will have been established between the couple during the passionate stage. If this is the case it will prevent the relationship from progressing into the compassionate and more secure stage.

By the same token a couple may never be able to move to this compassionate stage because they find that beyond sex and the passionate 'entertainment' there are few, if any, common interests between them and neither their personalities nor their interests relate to each other. Once the excitement of the sexual side settles down they will invariably find themselves with little to say or do with one another. At this point the relationship can only progress if a real conscious effort is made, on both sides, to take the relationship forward, in a form that allows both partners to enter the compassionate stage together. Otherwise it will stagnate and the couple will find it is not moving forward. Feelings will change and one or other will decide to bring it to an end.

For a relationship to remain healthy there has to be the right combination and balance of physical, intellectual, psychological, spiritual and sexual attraction between couples. Sometimes not all of these areas are present in a relationship; it may be that some of these aspects are not relevant for a couple. However, there will need to be enough of what is relevant to the couple for the relationship to survive and move on into the compassionate stage. This balance is often easier to achieve in non-AS couples as each partner's relationship needs are likely to be similar. However, in the case of the AS/non-AS relationship the areas that are relevant to each partner are likely to vary greatly as each will have very different needs.

In some cases the woman feels that it is an all or nothing situation with her partner; one minute he is making her feel as if she is the best thing that has ever happened in his life, the next she finds him behaving as though he is single and unattached, making her feel suddenly redundant in his life, as his focus shifts to something else, such as his work or a particular personal interest. So why does this happen?

It is not easy for an AS man to meet someone that matches the criteria he has in mind for a partner. Some men will have a very clear and definite checklist in their minds of the kind of woman they are looking for, how she should look or the qualities she will need to possess. What they are looking for will depend on the aspects most relevant to them. For some men it will be their intellect, for others it may be their spiritual beliefs and so on. When the AS man does meet the woman he is looking for, where all the boxes are ticked in the right places, then he will dedicate tremendous time, effort and planning to make it work between them.

He will be working hard in an effort to slot himself into her world and do the things she enjoys – in effect he will step outside of his own environment, his comfort zone, to achieve this. However, he will not be able to keep up this amount of effort for too long and will, once it feels safe enough, or when he feels the woman is enraptured, need to revert to his usual self, returning to his own environment and comfort zone. I explain why this happens in *The Asperger Couple's Workbook* (Aston 2008, pp.15–16) with my explanation of the species theory; for those who have not read it let me describe it again here.

Imagine the animal kingdom and its different species, which tend to be quite clearly defined, where each animal recognises others that are of the same species. Animal species tend not to mix with one another; lions mate with other lions, elephants other elephants; animals accept and know where they belong. It is unlikely that a lion will try to mate with an elephant or that an eagle will be found flirting with a zebra.

These pairings would simply not work, as both have very different dietary and environmental requirements to survive. A zebra could not exist on the top of a mountain with her beautiful eagle, as she would find the diet of raw meat her eagle thrives on not to her taste, while the eagle would find it difficult to survive amongst a herd of zebras munching grass all day, as he would more than likely either be trampled upon or die of malnutrition.

For my analogy of animals to people and relationships, consider how different species of animals require specific foods and environmental conditions if they are to thrive, which are determined by the species they belong to. If two people belong to the same species, they will have a good chance of a relationship working together. However, we humans have no way of knowing whether a person we meet and are attracted to does in reality belong to the same species as ourselves. People do, though, in their desire to believe they have found their life partner or soul mate, convince themselves and their partner that they are of the same species and are simply made for each other. Over time they may discover that they are in fact very different to each other and not of the same species at all.

To elaborate upon this concept, let us imagine that the AS male is an eagle and the AS female is a zebra. They have met and fallen in love; he is besotted by her and wants her to be with him, wants her to share his love and life. However, to do this he has to come out of his environment into hers. He has to fly down to the grasslands and live like a zebra; he will need to participate in zebra-like social events, meet her friends and family, interact and share communication on a regular basis, and he will be living in her environment and sharing her food.

To do this the AS man, just like the eagle, will have to come out of his comfort zone and survive in an unstructured, unpredictable environment that uses up every ounce of energy he has. Metaphorically he is temporarily in danger of being trampled upon and overwhelmed by the difference in environment. On top of this he is starving to death, which means his time is limited in this zebra environment. He will eventually have to fly back to his mountain, spend time alone and revitalise himself with his carnivorous diet, which for him is his sustenance. Eagle's survival time in zebra's environment is somewhat limited by the significant differences; there is no choice for him as, although he's making a supreme effort, zebra's world is slightly alien.

The trouble is that zebra will be totally unaware of the extreme effort and sacrifice he has been making to win her over to have her become part of his life. Consequently she will be devastated and deeply hurt when his attention moves away from her, especially as she will have no idea why. This is unlikely to ever be resolved through talking with one another for, when she asks him to explain, he will not be able to find the right words to make her feel reassured that he still really cares for her. This may be due to either his fear of confrontation or his difficulty with communicating his feelings.

Unfortunately, when there is a lack of awareness that Asperger syndrome is responsible for some of the difficulties the couple may be experiencing, it is likely that the relationship will begin to suffer and struggle. Things could become quite volatile between the couple and just as she will feel rejected and undervalued, he is likely to feel he is unappreciated, constantly criticised and as if he cannot do right for doing wrong. Feelings of confusion and resentment and, for some men, an extreme fear of any emotional confrontation, may become dominant within their relationship. He may feel used, abused and taken for granted – these feelings will all have had a profound effect upon his self-esteem. There will be many questions he would like to ask his partner, many things about her he does not understand, but he struggles with both. Having Asperger syndrome may make it very difficult for him to put himself in her shoes and it is unlikely that he will have made the connection between his behaviour and her reaction.

The aim of the next part of this book is to attempt to explain the logic and reason behind some of his behaviour, so he can develop a better understanding of himself, and I also try to answer some of the questions that he may have wanted to ask his partner about their relationship but has found himself quite unable to.

Rule 4

Always remember, women
are not rocket science!

9

Why are women so complicated?

The straight answer is that women are not complicated, especially when it comes down to what they need to make them happy in a relationship. In reality it is actually only simple and often small things that are needed to make women feel happy and secure within a relationship. The idea that women are not that difficult to please is unlikely to fit in with an Asperger perception, as many AS men will have already assumed that women are the most complicated creatures on the planet. In some ways this perceived complexity is not necessarily wrong, as women can be emotional and emotions are very complex. However, what women actually want from a man is quite straightforward and not complicated in the least.

To explain what seems to be something of a contradiction, I would like to use an example of an analogue watch. The internal workings of an analogue watch are made up of many tiny components that need to fit very precisely together to make it work accurately: tiny cogwheels, held together by delicate and intricate mechanisms and connections. Although the watch is obviously a complex and sophisticated device, all it takes to make this miracle of an invention work and keep time is a tiny little spring, wound with ease, by a small wheel on the side of the watch. This analogy can be applied to lots of things, such as a radio, a computer, a television or even the engine of a car. All are complex in construction, yet all are easily operated by a dial, a mouse, a button or a key.

So, yes, women are highly complex, especially within the realm of emotions; however, they are also relatively simple in what they require from their partner to make them happy. A woman's needs are so subtle that they are, more often than not, totally missed by the high performing logical Asperger brain, which is programmed to make sense of complex structures or fix misconfigurations. The AS man will take time to observe, analyse, process and interpret his partner's behaviour, looking for logical answers and labels, in an effort to help him make sense of her emotions, which he has probably realised by now appear to be completely illogical. Her emotions will be like a minefield to him and he will find himself treading very carefully in order to avoid possible confrontation.

Often he will be so busy and so absorbed in trying to work out what exactly she means or wants from him, that he will miss the moment or opportunity to interact effectively with his partner. It may be as innocuous as an opportunity to give her a hug, or for him to offer a listening ear without necessarily trying to fix a problem, or maybe she just wanted him to say something nice to make her feel worthwhile, such as reassuring her that she is loved by him.

He will miss these opportunities as his focus will be on fixing, when in fact she has not asked him to fix anything. When this happens she will potentially feel uncared for and unloved, especially if she does not know about Asperger syndrome. She will not understand why he ignored her look, her hints or her body language, which were all telling him to do something else, such as a give her a hug.

Imagine the AS man returning home from work, after quite a hard day, to find her banging pots around in the kitchen, showing obvious signs that she is not happy about something. He observes her behaviour and stands at the door, expressionless and without speaking, while trying to work out what he should do. He does not want to say anything about her obvious frustration for fear that it is him she is frustrated with, which might lead to a confrontation. He decides he is best to stick with what he would normally say, ignoring the fact that she is now leaning up against the kitchen sink, with her head down sobbing into a limp tea towel. He asks her (in his most unemotional tone) what time she would like to have dinner. In response to this question, which to her is cold, uncaring and a total denial of her feelings, she replies angrily, 'You have not got any dinner, I have only just returned from my mother's!'

His worst fear of confrontation starts to materialise; she is angry and he is feeling under attack. From her point of view he really should, having recognised that something had obviously upset her, have said something like, 'It sounds like you have had a really bad day. Let's have a hug and you can tell me all about it.' That response would be the simple version and a very quick way to diffuse her frustration, allow her to tell him what had gone on and have a good cry on his shoulder, the consequence being that she would have felt listened to, supported, cared for and loved. A non-AS guy might have been able to give her this, or something similar that would have been equally calming, taking the edge off the situation.

Without the capacity to sense or figure out that her frustration was not about him, the response from the man with AS could be quite defensive because he would have sensed her anger. He would be looking for an escape route or a solution. He would therefore either walk away, leaving her feeling abandoned, or, in an oddly defensive way, counterattack with something like, 'Well, perhaps you should not have stayed at your mother's so long and you would have been back in time to cook dinner.' Both of these responses would add fuel to the fire of the situation and result in both partners feeling hurt, attacked and unsupported.

In such situations the AS man will have picked up on her negative emotions, such as disappointment or anger; he will be aware that something is wrong but will not be able to work out what it is, or what he should do about it. He will instantly suspect it is something he has done, or not done, while being very aware that as far as he is concerned, he has not in any way intentionally tried to hurt or offend her. Based on this he will draw the conclusion that she is being unreasonable or just looking to criticise or pick a fight – he will probably either show his irritation or more likely make a decision to walk away, or say and do nothing for fear of further confrontation. Whichever of these three he decides upon, his partner will feel even more rejected and let down. His walking away will be, in her perception, a confirmation that he meant to hurt her as he is not even bothered or willing to talk about it. She will now either walk away too, burst into tears or find her hurt turns into anger, follow him demanding an explanation, which he is unlikely to be able to offer.

To the AS man this type of occurrence can feel overwhelming and confusing. He will struggle to make sense of it and is very likely to draw the conclusion that she is finding fault with him and that she is attacking him. This is usually not the case. No one is particularly to blame when this happens; just as it was not his intention to hurt her, neither was it her intention to appear critical or aggressive.

Men in general find it more difficult than women to read the perspective of their partner. In trials of mindreading tests, women were often found to score higher than men. It is widely accepted that the female brain tends to be more right-side dominant, whereas the male brain will tend to be left-side dominant. The male brain may be excellent at applying linear processing or being spatially aware or systematising, strengths the female brain may be less adept at. However, empathetic thought and intuition are certainly strengths the female brain has over the male. So mindreading issues will occur in any relationship but not to the same extreme they will occur when Asperger syndrome is brought into the equation. Being affected by AS will exaggerate this problem and often hinder future learning from situations.

Incidents like this can be avoided if the AS man can learn to switch off his propensity to look to find a solution and an assumption of guilt turning to defensiveness. In many incidents it is the reaction that overly complicates the issue as opposed to the actual issue itself. For example, if the AS man was attending a workshop or learning a new task at work, and was not sure what the person teaching him wanted him to do, he would not normally walk out of the room or become defensive with them. He would simply ask them what it is they require him to do, or to show him how to work it out. This is the same approach that needs to be applied to his partner and she needs to be asked what it is that is bothering or upsetting her. If she understands Asperger syndrome, she will understand that he needs her to verbalise and explain her needs.

Of course, there is no guarantee this will always work and much will be dependent on the situation and the reason she is upset. It is, though, a starting point to resolving issues and if she understands the effects of AS, she will see it as an attempt by the man to work things out and show he cares.

Probably the most important thing for the AS man to remember is that, unless his partner has asked him directly to solve a problem for her, he should resist the urge to try to fix it for her, even if he believes he has found the solution. He will need to keep reminding himself that for the majority of the time she just needs a hug, a kind word or a listening ear; all things that he is able to give her − it's really as simple as that.

10

I feel that whatever I do it will be wrong, especially when she is upset. If I say nothing it is wrong, if I say something that will be wrong too. So is it all my fault?

The short answer to this question is no; relationships are about the interaction between two people and unless one partner is intentionally trying to hurt or abuse the other, there can never be a time when all the blame can be placed on one partner alone. There will, though, be periods in all relationships, regardless of whether one partner has AS, when the feeling between the couple will be that neither can do right for doing wrong. This is often a consequence of a build up of issues and grievances between the couple.

If a partner is feeling resentful and this builds up it can negate their judgement and they will unconsciously interpret everything the other does as wrong, frustrating or deliberately malicious. In non-AS relationships this is often the point where both would acknowledge that things were not going well and the couple might agree to try to talk about their problems together. From this they might decide to go to couple counselling or try to find ways to see things from the other's perspective and negotiate and compromise their differences.

In relationships where one partner has AS it is unlikely that the problems will be acknowledged and dealt with in the same way as in a non-AS couple, as the AS man will be doing everything in his power to avoid confrontation and one way of doing this will be to deny anything is wrong and ignore the differences between them. He is not going to be able to understand her perspective and figure out that the reason she is upset or angry is because she feels unloved by him and hurt that he does not seem to take her pleas seriously. She may be unaware that his silence is not an indication of lack of caring but because Asperger syndrome makes it difficult for him to read the deeper levels of her emotional response.

To make things worse, if she does try to discuss the issues, he may well interpret her words as a direct criticism of him, rather than her attempt to improve things between them, and the result will be that he will withdraw even more. He will become more distant and hence she will become more emotionally demanding, which will cause him to become even more distant. He will not work out the repetition of this pattern of unresolved issues, as his priority will be avoiding confrontation, not realising it is this very avoidance that is causing it. Fear of getting it wrong and the possibility of causing a confrontation is one of the main reasons that AS men will choose not to communicate with or give an opinion to their partners.

It is imperative that the couple find help to sort this out, whether it is by increasing their understanding of the effects of Asperger syndrome on both of them, or by going to see a counsellor with an understanding of AS. His partner will need to change the way she is communicating with him, and rather than expect him to guess how she feels she will need to be more direct in her communication, explaining clearly and in a non-judgemental way why she is upset or angry and what it is she wants him to do to support her. Most importantly, she will need to make it safe for him to ask questions and check out what she wants him to do in the knowledge that there will not be an angry reaction. He, likewise, will need to learn that it is OK to ask questions and that walking away or ignoring the situation exacerbates it and only results in making things worse for him in the long run.

11

I get to a point that I feel I want to run away, as I cannot discuss or argue any more. Why won't she just let me go?

Wanting to run away, go to sleep or find somewhere alone is called the flight response. It is the opposite of the fight response, which can appear quite volatile and threatening. It does seem that a majority of men with AS belong in the passive group and respond to confrontation with a flight response. Going into flight is for the majority of men with AS a survival strategy that they apply when their stress levels become too high. Part of this is to do with personalities as well as being affected by AS.

Asperger syndrome does not change personality: it will not make a person nice, nasty, good or bad. It will cause a difficulty in the area of social interaction, communication and applying empathetic thought; how this shows itself in the relationship will also depend on the person's characteristics. AS seems to exaggerate characteristics and personality traits and if the person's personality is passive and non-reactive then having AS will make it more so. Likewise the same will happen if the personality type is reactive; in either case the reaction will be triggered by an increase in stress levels and when these become too high the AS person will either go into fight or flight. This is often explained as overload or meltdown.

The majority of men I work with are quite passive by nature and I encourage their flight response as being by far the better option and less damaging than the fight response. The fight response can feel very threatening and intimidating for partners and family, and cause hurt feelings and problems for all involved. I have worked with AS clients who have lost jobs, friends and partners because of it. However, the flight response does also come with potential drawbacks as far as the relationship is concerned.

Flight is like turning off a computer; it is lights out and complete shutdown. In reality it often means doing and saying nothing at all and this reaction can be very misunderstood by the female partner if she does not understand the reasons behind it. Unfortunately the flight response often occurs at a time when the female partner is very eager to sort out and resolve the issues that have risen by discussion and compromise. So just when his partner wants to talk and resolve the issues she will find he has lost all powers to communicate, has completely shut down and will not be able to discuss anything. It is likely, if she does not understand Asperger syndrome, that this to her will feel like a rejection and a sign that he does not care enough to talk it over, when the reality is that he has no choice and is no longer able to find the words to communicate and discuss anything.

Female brains appear to be wired differently to men's and their way of solving problems is to talk them over, to be open about emotions and to have deep meaningful conversations. Men, on the whole, can sometimes struggle with this; for AS men it is almost impossible and even more so if they are also affected by alexithymia. Alexithymia is a Greek word which simply means 'no words for feelings' (Parker, Taylor and Bagby 2001). It affects approximately 85 per cent of people affected by AS (Hill, Berthoz and Frith 2004) and is largely responsible for the difficulties AS men often have in expressing emotions.

If the effect of alexithymia is understood by both partners there are ways that can be explored to compensate for the lack of words; for example, some AS men find they are far more able to express their feelings in emails or text messages. With this understanding a couple can use a medium that does not involve verbal communication to work through their issues. If, however, there is no awareness, acceptance or understanding of the impacts of AS and alexithymia then refusal to discuss emotions will be taken very personally by the woman. This is understandable if it is her belief that he could talk to her if he wanted to. If she believes this then she will feel that he is punishing her or not valuing her enough to make the effort, which will leave her feeling hurt and defensive.

If this breakdown in communication is happening in a relationship and the AS man is finding himself constantly walking away from his partner or avoiding any discussion with her over it, then he will need to help his partner understand why. This may be better achieved with the help of an experienced counsellor, who in the safety of the counselling room will enable the couple to discuss the issues between them. If this is not an option then it may help to develop a better understanding of AS and alexithymia by reading more on the subject and exploring together how they might find better ways to communicate without the threat of confrontation.

She will need to understand that if her partner has reached overload then he needs to be proffered the time to go somewhere quiet and alone to give his brain time to catch up with the backlog of information he has yet to process in order that he may regain control over his thoughts and mental processes. Realising that her partner has no choice over this should help her to change her perception over the reasons he withdraws. However, it will be very important for her that this means the discussion is simply postponed and not avoided altogether, which would result in the accumulation of a mass of undiscussed and unresolved issues.

12

She asks me what I feel or why I love her and before I can answer she has become reactive/angry/upset/critical. Why?

Within couple counselling it is not uncommon for a counsellor to ask the couple at some point whether they love each other and for each partner to consider and describe what it is they love about the other. This is an exercise that can offer benefits to each as they reflect on the meaning of their love for the other. However, in the case of a non-AS/AS couple the conversation with the counsellor is likely to be as follows:

Therapist 'Do you love John, Mary?'

Mary [answering instantly] 'Yes, I do very much.'

Therapist 'Why do you love him?'

Mary [promptly answering again] 'Because he looks after me, he is safe and secure, he is faithful and loyal. I know he tries his best to please me, and yes, I also find him very attractive and fancy him like crazy!'

Therapist 'And you, John, do you love Mary?'

John looks away, stares at the table and appears to be deep in thought. This continues and John still does not reply. After a couple of minutes of silence Mary is beginning to look upset.

John 'Well, yes, I suppose I must do.'

Therapist 'Can you tell us what it is about Mary you love, John?'

John takes a deep breath and is again lost in thought. A few more minutes pass in silence. Mary's body language has changed from being quite relaxed and contented to becoming tense and showing obvious signs of feeling hurt.

John [eventually] 'Because she is attractive and a good mother.'

Mary [now with tears in her eyes and shouting] 'Was it that hard to decide whether you love me? You even struggled to think of a reason why you love me. Attractive! Good mother! Is that the best thing you could come up with? I can't believe it took you so long to answer!'

The scene above is not uncommon and illustrates one of the misinterpretations that frequently occurs between AS/non-AS couples. This misunderstanding is caused by the difference in how each will process information and formulate a reply when being asked to consider and describe their feelings. It will often take the AS partner much longer to answer a question about their feelings than it will take the non-AS partner, because each will be using a different part of the brain to articulate their feelings and give an answer to the question. Unless the AS partner already has a formulated script it will take him much longer to answer questions about his feelings. Unfortunately, this hesitation and delay in answering is often misunderstood by the non-AS partner, who will mistakenly read this as him being unsure or deceitful, and if her partner was not on the spectrum then she would probably be right.

The reason for the delay in answering a question which is about his feelings is because the answer is being processed in the brain via the logical route rather than being processed by theory of mind, which would be able to decide and respond as quickly as answering a simple mathematical equation such as what two plus two equals. Logic could answer this in a flash; however, questions which are about feelings take much longer for an answer to be processed, formulated and quality controlled before a spoken answer can safely be given.

The majority of women are encouraged from an early age to acknowledge their feelings and discuss them, and the woman will be quite used to working on an emotional level and having a library of emotional responses already stored in her memory banks. Her ability to dive into her emotions and describe them instantly is almost second nature to her, which is why she may struggle to understand why her partner is so different to her.

In addition to a difference in processing which will cause the time delay, it might also be the case that the AS partner is affected by alexithymia, which will make it almost impossible to find the right words to describe his feelings. If this is the case and she does not understand this then she is bound to feel hurt and unloved when an answer is not forthcoming.

Having AS will mean having to think the answer through logically and the time this takes is not an indication of whether the person is being genuine or does not feel love or have feelings. However, without this knowledge and understanding her defensive reaction is not surprising; once she understands this it should make a difference to her reaction.

In other cases, however, the delay in answering questions about his feelings may be because the man is afraid that he will get it wrong and this fear will be based on a past history of him doing just that. It may be that in the past the AS man has given a very honest opinion; for example, she may have asked him if he thought she should lose weight, to which he had responded yes. His answer may have been honest, but it may not be well received by the woman and may be interpreted as being insensitive. Her hurt feelings will result in either tears or feelings of anger towards him and he will probably not have a clue what it is he has said or done wrong. Over time he will lose trust in his ability to give the right answer and trust in his partner's reaction to his answer. The consequence of this is that he would have misguidedly learned that no reply would have been the safer alternative.

If an AS man finds he is really struggling with describing to his non-AS partner how he feels about her then first he needs to let her know that this is not because he doesn't feel anything or is unsure of how he feels about her. It is simply that having AS or being affected by alexithymia makes it so difficult. His partner may find that if he is asked how much he loves her out of 10 (10 being the most love) he is able to give a more accurate and speedier response.

It is all about making the AS partner feel safe. If we were talking about a person who was affected by dyslexia whose partner got upset or angry every time they misspelled a word, then that person would soon refuse to write anything down for fear of the repercussions they would suffer when at some point they inevitably spelled a word wrong. Another similarity between dyslexia and Asperger syndrome is that if the person affected by either is put under pressure or feeling stressed then they will be more likely to make a mistake or say the wrong thing.

If the female wishes her partner to discuss his feelings then she will need to choose her time carefully, when things are calm, and she is not putting him under any unnecessary pressure. In addition there will need to be an acceptance by her that her partner may find it easier to show his love by doing things for her and his family rather than expressing his love in words and emotions. Some men work very hard to support their family and this is sometimes taken for granted. The fact is, this way of showing his love can sadly often go unnoticed and unappreciated.

13

She tells me I have a communication problem, yet I have been complimented on my communication at work. Who is right here?

I have worked with university lecturers, project managers, consultants, teachers and politicians who have an excellent job record and show little evidence of having any difficulty in communicating; however, their partners would complain that they rarely had a conversation together and that he would come home from work and never even think to ask her about her day or how she was when he saw her.

Women often express their confusion over why their partner can, for example, talk at a conference to hundreds of people and yet not sit down with them and converse unless it is about something he was interested in. She would argue that the second she tried to discuss her feelings, their parents, the children or the relationship she would be faced with a mute blank stare. I talked earlier about the differences in how the brain of a person with AS works in comparison to the brain of a non-AS person and described how there is, for the AS partner, a leaning towards the logical side of the brain in preference to the empathetic side of the brain.

When an AS person is talking at work it is likely to be about a work-based topic; for instance, an accountant will have many conversations about tax laws, balance sheets, annual returns, turnover and profit. It is unlikely they will be discussing the feelings of their co-workers or describing how upset they are over last night's fallout with their wife. The conversations they have at work will only require that they use the logical part of the brain.

It is also the case that, for many AS men, their work will probably also be their special interest, so it will be a topic they will know inside out and be very confident in discussing.

This, though, is very different to what they will be faced with when they walk through the door of their family home, where they will often be faced with a cocktail of chaos, emotions, excitement and multiple distractions and find in a very short time their brains are overloaded with the sensory input around them. Even if their home life is quite organised and quiet the AS man may still be faced with a partner who wants to discuss topics on a very different emotional level than the topics he has left behind at work.

Sharing information, feelings and concerns is a fundamental part of the non-AS partner's needs. This is due to the difference in how the non-AS partner's brain works. She, unlike him, will find that at the end of a busy day she is now in need of a break from the conversations and stress endured throughout the day. It may be that she has had a really bad day and needs to share it; she may have had only the children to converse with all day and is now in need of adult conversation about adult topics. She wants to talk to someone who understands her feelings, who will ask about her day and share in an emotional context what has gone on for each of them. To do this the female partner will be using theory of mind and engaging the emotional part of her brain. She will be able to engage with spontaneity different emotions, drawing from a well-equipped library of emotional feelings, expressions and thoughts. For her this is chill out time and she will be unaware that for her AS partner this will be major stress time and the last thing he needs at the end of a busy day.

It is important to remember here that no one is right or wrong: it is about each partner having different needs. This difference can be settled and compromised when it is understood by both that it is not a personal issue. The difference is not due to the AS man choosing not to communicate on an emotional level, as often, due to Asperger syndrome, he does not have a choice. Neither is it the case that she is unjustifiably attacking him, being critical or trying to make life difficult for him by putting these emotional demands on him, because emotional communication is for her a fundamental and necessary requirement in her life.

One way of compromise is for the AS man to be offered 30 minutes' (or longer if possible) private time before having to enter into relevant communication. This time could be used by him either to be alone, listen to music or be involved in something that he enjoys. These 30 minutes would allow his brain time to make the transition from work mode to home mode in his head. Unlike her, he is unable just to switch off and leave his day behind; he will need to file away the residue of information he is carrying in his brain in order to have enough space to allow other topics, such as absorbing her day, to come in.

After the 30 minutes (or whatever amount of time has been agreed) he can then join his partner and family and allow them to discuss their day, and if he wishes he can discuss his too. I do, though, recommend that all major or sensitive topics are not discussed until the couple are alone and there are no distractions from television, family or telephones.

14

I feel like she purposely pushes me until I react and then acts the victim and blames me for getting angry. Why does she do this?

The reason she does this is twofold: (1) she is looking for some sign of emotion from her partner, in whatever form that takes, and (2) she wants to get his attention. The reason for this is that AS men can find it very difficult to express their emotions and if they are also affected by alexithymia, as so many are, then it is likely that this lack of emotional expression will be even more exaggerated.

I discovered that the women in my research often took on a rescuer role at the beginning of the relationship. This was not because the AS man had asked to be rescued; quite the opposite. It is more about the nature of the women who men with AS seem to be attracted to and choose to be their partners. My research found that the majority of women that AS men were attracted to were emotional, nurturing, empathetic women who often worked in the caring professions. It is as though they chose a woman at the other end of the spectrum to themselves: women who could compensate for what they lacked in the social field.

This type of woman will often sense in the AS man childlike qualities and a passive and gentle nature which does not lend itself to spontaneous emotional outbursts of excitement or passion. She will be attracted to these childlike qualities and experience him as quiet, considerate and a gentleman, quite unlike the more sexually focused men she may have encountered in the past. When, over time, she finds his lack of emotional affect does not change, it is likely that she will blame this on some aspect of his childhood, for example, the fact he went to boarding school or had parents who were not demonstrative or emotional.

She will believe that underneath his silent unemotional demeanour is a passionate and emotional man trying to discover himself and get out. She will unconsciously seek to rescue him, to teach him how to show his feelings; she will believe that she can do this by offering him emotional expression and love and she will be doing this in the hope that it will eventually be reciprocated. Of course, she will not be doing this consciously or in any way to manipulate him; it will all be happening on a very unconscious level and neither will be fully aware of the dynamics that are being played out in the relationship.

However, over a period of time, often years, it will start to become apparent to her that things are not going to change, that, no matter how hard she tries, he is still not discussing either her feelings or his with her. She is still not being offered any emotional expression and will begin to interpret this as him not caring enough to say or show her how he feels about her. She will start to become more and more frustrated; resentment will start to build up, and when this happens in a relationship it will soon become apparent that everything he does or does not do will irritate her or cause a reaction. She will find herself becoming a person she is not; she will start to become angry and unfortunately find herself picking on everything he does.

He, meanwhile, will have no idea what is going on or why things have changed from how they used to be. In the past he will have become accustomed to how much she showered him with love and affection, but will have presumed that she did this because she wanted to, because it made her happy. He will not at any point have considered that it was because she wanted him to do the same back; after all if she just wanted a hug why did she not ask him?

During her journey from rescuer to persecutor it is probable that she will have asked her partner to share and discuss his feelings with her and, in the beginning, he may have tried to do this. However, he is likely to have learned from experience that to get his answers right is a rarity; he is more likely to get it wrong and this upsets her and causes a confrontation. To avoid the consequences of a confrontation he will have learned not to say anything at all or to avoid the subject of feelings if they come up. Unfortunately, this silent response will result in making her even needier of his emotional expression and will increase the frustration she feels even more. This is the point in the relationship in which she will start to flip from rescuer to persecutor, as she will discover that the latter is more likely to receive an emotional response.

In many cases, though, he will not respond, and will just walk away, which will cause her to become even more attacking or verbal. However, even the most placid man may eventually react with anger if pushed far enough and for too long. In addition, not all men with AS are placid and for men whose response to stress is fight rather than flight, the response will be reactive and defensive: he will equal her verbal attacks and may become aggressive in his body language. The AS man will be giving her an emotional reaction which at least to her is a reaction and, no, it is not the reaction she originally wanted, but it is emotional; she has got his attention and he will have given her the excuse to vent all her pent up frustration onto him.

When I see relationships that have reached this level of dysfunctional behaviour, the couple will have in most cases been together for a long time, sometimes many years. It will have taken a lot of heartache on her part before this state is reached. For some of the couples I see it is too late and too much damage has been caused by verbal abuse and threats. For many, though, I find that once an understanding is reached on why and how this pattern developed, once both have a clear understanding of how each other's brain works differently, and most importantly, once she understands that anger is a useless emotion in this relationship, then, and only then, remarkable changes can be made to the relationship.

It takes a long time for a relationship to reach this level of dysfunction, and it can be prevented if the issues are addressed early enough. If, though, the AS man finds himself in a relationship where he feels constantly attacked or provoked, he must see it as a sign that both need help and accept that avoiding or denying the situation is not going to make it go away. In fact it will make it worse. He will need to approach his partner and tell her that he wants to work at the relationship, as he is aware that neither of them is happy. He could suggest counselling for both of them.

If, however, he feels unable to approach her like this he could try putting it in an email or letter and sending it to her in his absence to allow her time to consider his feelings. It is important that he lets her know he wants things to change and improve and is willing to try his best. If, though, he finds that despite his genuine efforts his partner is not willing to try to make things better it may be time for both to consider the value of the relationship.

15

Why is she always criticising me?

This issue comes up in every relationship I have worked with and I hear often from the AS man that he feels constantly put down, picked on and criticised by his partner. Some will go as far as to say that all she ever seems to do is criticise them, and that whatever they do or however hard they try, she will still hold them culpable for just about everything.

The message I receive from the women is often the opposite, as they will express the feeling that whatever they say to the man, regardless of whether it is well meaning or supportive, he will become defensive and will interpret it as criticism of him. Many women go on to explain that even if they are trying to improve the relationship or suggest ways that might make things easier for him, he still reads it as critical and assumes that they are picking fault with him.

For example, the woman might suggest to her partner that if he tries to do something in a different way, it could make things easier for him. Unfortunately, he might interpret this as her saying that he has been getting things wrong all this time, which for him will feel like he is being told he has failed again! He will be left feeling criticised, undermined and that she has been deceiving him in the past by pretending that everything was OK. His reaction to this could be defensive and within no time the couple could find themselves in a heated debate, which will leave her feeling unjustifiably challenged and misunderstood when she was simply trying to make things better for him. Likewise, he will be left feeling unjustifiably criticised and equally misunderstood.

Women will often report that they feel they spend the majority of their time walking on eggshells and dread having to discuss any personal or family issues with their partner. They add in despair that they have tried so many times to talk to him and to convey the message in as friendly and non-threatening a way as they could, and still he reacts defensively and accuses them of attacking him. He, on the other hand, will be left with the belief that whatever he does his partner finds fault with him and will use every available opportunity to put him down.

So why such a major deviation between a couple when both are describing the same relationship? Is one partner being dishonest? Is one right in their perception of the situation while the other is wrong? The answer to both these questions is a big no: both are being honest in describing their perception and both are right in their description of how it makes them feel.

Understanding the underlying message that is being expressed in communication requires the ability to read another person's non-verbal body language. Often it is just a look in the eyes that tells us whether a person is being honest, dishonest, supportive or critical; this look might only last a microsecond, so picking up on the meaning of the look requires a very rapid interpretation; otherwise it is just the words that will be heard and processed. The words taken alone without the extra information that the body is transmitting can be easily misunderstood, as can the motives of the person delivering the message.

It is this misinterpretation of the intent of the non-AS partner by the AS partner that causes him to feel wrongly criticised and attacked. This is caused by his difficulty in reading her body language accurately. Mindreading is an area that Asperger syndrome can make very difficult to achieve; in many cases had he been able to read his partner's body language it would have told him she was trying to be supportive and offer positive criticism, not the negative he read it to be. If neither in the relationship understands the reason why this miscommunication continuously occurs between them they will only blame each other. They will be unaware that they cannot presume that they have been read or have read the other accurately, and continue to form false and negative assumptions over what they believe has been communicated. Of course, there will be times when she is being critical of him, just as he will at times criticise her and, if this is the case, it must be made clear so that it can be dealt with as best the couple are able to do.

His feelings of being criticised can impact on many areas of the relationship, including the sexual side. An example is that she may suggest he touches her in a different way; he might feel that she is saying he has been touching her incorrectly in the past and that he has been deceived into believing that she was satisfied and pleased with his performance in bed.

Another example of this misinterpretation is if she talks about someone else who has achieved well in their career or even done well in a project in their home, such as when one woman informed her partner that her brother in law had put in a whole new kitchen for her sister and he had done a fantastic job. He may instantly feel that she was comparing him unfavourably to her brother in law and making him feel criticised and useless! His reaction to this will be to become defensive and reactive. Once again, before they know it, the couple find they are falling out with each other. This will leave both feeling misunderstood and attacked, and what could have been a positive and constructive conversation becomes a negative and unnecessary argument.

A way to be sure of the intention of another is to respond to their statement with a question rather that react with a counterattack. If he simply asks his partner whether her comment was meant as a personal criticism or if it was intended as an attempt to be supportive or helpful, then, one hopes, she will answer honestly. If her answer is no, she is not trying to criticise him or put him down, then he must believe her and hear her out. In the majority of cases the non-AS partner is, just like him, wanting to be happy and improve the relationship. Both want what is best for each other, themselves and the relationship. It is important that both partners are able to talk without either becoming defensive. This is the only way that issues will be resolved, allowing both to make improvements and move on.

However, if anyone finds themselves in a relationship where they are constantly and intentionally put down, criticised or verbally abused they will have to decide what is best for them. For some that is to walk away and cease all communication until their partner can talk to them in a civil and respectful way. No one should have to accept being spoken to in a derogatory way. If this fails to satisfy then they may want to consider if the relationship is right for them and has their best interests at heart. Both have equal rights in the relationship and both have the right to be spoken to in a way that is respectful.

Rule 5

If you are in company and she exaggerates an issue, do not correct her — ever!

16

Why does she exaggerate so often?

To explain why this happens I shall describe a typical scenario, once again using the pseudonyms John and Mary.

John and Mary had arrived at their counselling session and were both describing the events that had occurred over the previous weekend together, which had caused a major fallout between them. I had been surprised by this, as until this point the couple had been working really well together, and had managed to overcome most of their differences and develop a good understanding of each other.

I first asked John what had caused the row between them, to which he replied that he did not really know as, in his opinion, he felt nothing had gone wrong. John described how they had been to an annual dinner dance with Mary's office colleagues. Everything seemed OK until they returned home, when Mary went absolutely mad at him, saying she would never ever take him anywhere again and that she had never felt so humiliated in her life. John said he could not get a word in edgeways and felt he was being attacked by her without justification. He could only assume she just needed an excuse to cause an altercation with him so she could vent all her frustration and anger. He said they had hardly spoken since and feels he is being punished for having AS.

I turned to Mary and asked if she could share her interpretation of the evening and what had caused her to be so upset with John. It did not come as a surprise to hear her describe the evening's events from a very different perspective to the way John had interpreted the situation. This difference in perspective is not uncommon in AS/non-AS relationships.

Mary described how the annual event had been organised by the legal firm she worked for as a solicitor. Mary enjoyed her job and was eager to work her way up and even hoped that she would soon be asked to join the company as a partner. Her employers had met John before and he had got on well with her work colleagues.

At the meal they had been placed on a table of eight, which included two of the company partners with their wives. When the subject, during conversation, of walking as good exercise was raised, Mary, a keen fell walker, was eager to tell of a recent trip they had made – of how they climbed Great Gable together, at 900 metres the ninth highest mountain in England. She went on to say they'd managed this in less than three hours. As she paused, about to continue, John interjected to say, 'Mary, Great Gable is 899 metres, it is the tenth highest mountain and we were nearer three and a half hours in getting up there.' Mary, left openmouthed and embarrassed by this correction, gathered herself together and continued her story.

Having Asperger syndrome can cause difficulties in understanding the difference between an exaggeration, elaboration, bragging or white lie and being knowingly deceitful or dishonest. All will come under the category of lying or getting the facts wrong in the black and white world of AS. John felt he had a duty to put it right and correct Mary on the facts. He was not attempting to undermine Mary, merely offer accuracy. There are no grey areas in this realm and, although this way of thinking has many benefits, it can also have its downsides in circumstances like the one I have just described.

People often make things sound more exciting than they were and will often uses exaggerations when describing something to do this. For example, they may say, 'There were hundreds of people on the bus today,' or they 'had to wait forever in the queue for the post office'. Neither of these are literal statements, however, to the Asperger brain, these are false facts and need to be corrected, otherwise they give the listener an inaccurate account.

It is unlikely the AS man will be able to persuade his partner not to use exaggerations, as this is a way of expressing herself without the intention to deceive; the specific details are trivial and their inaccuracy does not cause harm to anyone. The example given here of John and Mary's situation clearly illustrates that Mary meant no harm by elaborating on her story. Her intent was to make her story sound more exciting and impressive and, by the same token, John meant no harm by correcting the facts.

I explain to the AS partner how people express themselves, and that if he hears his partner being liberal with the truth or exaggerating, he should try to hold back on immediately correcting her. If he needs to say something he should wait until they are both alone, when she can explain the reason for elaborating. It is advisable for him not to correct her in front of other people, as this can cause her to feel embarrassed or humiliated.

It will not be easy for the AS man to change his reaction to inaccuracy and he may find himself still correcting her before he has even realised he is doing so. If this is the case and he cannot control his reaction then it will need to be her that makes the change. She can do this by telling her stories in his absence or, when telling a story, refer to him during the story to confirm the facts. However, if in time he is able to learn to follow the rule to be silent it will benefit both of them and the benefit will certainly outweigh the cost.

Rule 6

Lying is best avoided, as men with AS rarely make convincing liars!

17

If I keep quiet it is wrong and if I speak up it is wrong! Why?

It is understandable why the AS man becomes confused over this and he might feel at times that he cannot do right for doing wrong. It is only when Asperger honesty coupled with Asperger non-disclosure is truly understood that it will make sense to both partners in the relationship. It has been said that people with AS cannot lie; this is not exactly accurate, as someone with AS can consciously choose to deceive another person. Their honesty, though, is often highly dependent on what they perceive will be the consequences of telling the truth and being open.

The majority of men I see on the spectrum will do almost anything to avoid confrontation and will often lie by non-disclosure if it avoids the possibility of an argument. If, though, they are asked a very direct question for which they do not have a prepared script then they will almost inevitably state the truth, as the Asperger brain does not come equipped with the imagination to think up a lie quickly enough that would be convincing and that they could actually make sound convincing. When I am asked by a couple whether people with AS can choose to tell lies my answer will be, yes, someone with AS is perfectly capable of lying; however, their ability to lie will often be impaired.

The reason for being poor at lying comes down to an underdeveloped theory of mind. To be a good liar one has to be able to see things from the other person's perspective and to know what will convince them that you are telling the truth. Lying successfully often depends on using the right facial expressions, body language and tone of voice. Getting these things right will be almost impossible for most people on the spectrum as they will not be able to adjust the way they sound and look according to what the other person expects. So, just as someone with AS will find it difficult to tell when they are being deceived by reading another's body language, they will equally find it hard to deceive others themselves and will therefore rarely try. This may give their partner the false perception that they will be open and honest about everything.

Consequently, their partner will probably be very surprised to discover they have been dishonest; this could be over something trivial, such as not paying a bill on time, or it may be something major, such as being in a large amount of debt. It is more than likely that this deceit will have been due to non-disclosure on the part of the partner with AS and it will only have been when their partner had asked a very clear, direct and specific question that they either attempted to lie or, more usually, come out with the truth. For example, a question such as, 'Have you paid the credit card?' could receive an answer 'Yes,' which is totally honest. However, they could well omit the fact that they paid it late and have consequently been charged interest, for fear that this could cause an issue with their partner. If, though, she had then followed up her original question with, 'Did you pay the credit card on time?' then she would have been told the truth.

For some couples this non-disclosure can cause a major problem in their relationship and affect the level of trust she offers him. For example, one woman described how she took a day out to visit her parents who lived quite a distance away. Her father had been admitted to hospital and was quite poorly, and she wanted to spend some time visiting him and supporting her mother. It was a weekend, so she was able to leave the children, aged four and one, with their father. This was the first time she had left them for any amount of time, and she had provided her partner with a list of their needs, prepared food and snacks and a supply of nappies and wipes. She also asked him to make sure he kept his mobile on as they did not have a landline and she might need to get hold of him. He agreed and she left, reassuring herself that all would be well.

Just to satisfy herself and have some reassurance from him that all was going all right, she tried to call him throughout the day but found that his mobile just went straight to answerphone. As the day progressed she felt herself starting to panic and was not sure what to do. She called again; by now it was late in the afternoon, and she felt very relieved when this time he answered and she heard his voice. I will again call them John and Mary; the conversation went like this:

John 'Hello.'

Mary 'Oh John, thank goodness you have answered. I have been trying to call you all day.'

John 'I have had three missed calls from you at lunchtime.'

Mary 'Stop being pedantic, John! Why was your phone turned off? I asked you to keep it on.'

John [starting to feel defensive] 'My phone was not turned off!'

Mary [also getting frustrated] 'Yes it was, it went straight to answerphone!'

John [now becoming even more defensive and sounding very irate] 'No, it was not off and if you continue to attack me over this I shall end the call!'

Mary [deciding it is not worth pursuing the topic] 'How are the children? Have they been good? What are they doing?'

John [taking a deep breath] 'James is having a nap and Ami is watching CBeebies.'

Mary 'Have they had lunch?'

John 'Yes.'

Mary [picking up that John is still annoyed] 'Oh, OK then – I will go now. I will be home about seven o'clock, in time to say goodnight to them. See you later, call me if you need to. Bye my love.'

John 'Bye.'

Except for the dispute over John's phone being turned off all seemed fine to Mary. It was only when she arrived home and discovered that their young son had two stitches in his forehead that she became aware that something had obviously gone very wrong.

Mary 'What on earth has happened to James?'

John 'He cut his head. I took him to A&E. He has been checked and they said he is OK.'

Mary [feeling quite hysterical with John at this point] 'But why did you not call me or tell me about this when we spoke?'

John 'You did not ask! All you seemed to be bothered about was whether my phone had been turned off.'

As can be imagined, Mary was angry with John, and could make no sense of why he had not given her this information about their son when she phoned. It was only when the issue was raised in the counselling room that John felt able to explain his perception of the incident and she was able to understand.

John explained how James had fallen and caught his head on the corner of the coffee table. He had immediately driven them both to A&E and while they were at the hospital he had no signal on his phone. After his son was patched up and it was confirmed he was OK he took the children back home and put his son in his cot for his nap and put the television on for his daughter. When Mary called he felt she was angry with him and felt attacked by her accusations that he had turned his phone off. The last thing he wanted to do after this was to tell her about their son as he did not want to provoke her anger any more and cause a confrontation between them. John also added that it would be pointless telling Mary what had occurred as there would have been nothing she could do, and after all everything was OK and had all been dealt with.

This delaying of giving information comes up a lot in couple therapy and it is almost always due to the fear of confrontation:

rather than take the risk he omits to give her information. He will not consider this as lying or deceiving if his partner does not ask the question in a way that is specific enough to require an honest answer. Without being asked directly he will not see that he has told a lie; this way of logically justifying non-disclosure is not untypical when someone is affected by AS.

The intent behind this is not to deceive; it is to avoid her emotional reaction if he risked disclosing to her, as this would be very difficult for him to manage and respond to. The learning that the AS man needs to take on here is that delaying the passing on of 'irrelevant' information will only aggravate the situation and the delaying of this information will cause a far more reactive confrontation than would have occurred had he been upfront from the beginning. His non-disclosure will often result in an angrier reaction from her when she realises he kept relevant information from her.

When, though, he is asked a very specific question by her such as 'Do you like my new dress?' or 'Do you still find me desirable?' he will tell her the truth even if it hurts her, because, to his logical brain, why would she ask such a specific question if she did not want him to be honest? He will answer with the honesty and innocence of a child, completely unaware of the impact this honesty might have on the other person. Unfortunately, this is often how his non-disclosure begins, as realising he has upset her or made her angry will convince him that he needs to be very cautious as to how he answers her questions. Based on this it is not surprising that in my research I found that only 10 per cent of the men I spoke to felt comfortable disclosing information about themselves (Aston 2003).

These are issues that are likely to occur in all AS/non-AS relationships at some point, though they can often be resolved or at least better understood when both partners know and understand the effects of AS. The woman will learn from experience that if she does not want the truth, not to ask a question which would prompt it. Fortunately, most women come to appreciate this honesty and find it quite refreshing. They find that the openness and innocence of the AS man gives safeness to the relationship and they feel quite secure in the knowledge that as long as they ask the right question they will not be deceived. However, until this understanding is fully developed between the couple there are going to be many times when the AS man's honesty causes a confrontation. The danger is that avoidance and non-disclosure may become a way of life for him.

One way the man may attempt to avoid the possibility of a confrontation or upsetting his partner by giving his honest opinion to a personal question is to try tactics that will divert the responsibility to proffer an answer away from him. For example, if his partner asks him about her clothes or hairstyle and he knows his answer would not be a positive one, then admitting that he is not an expert on women's clothes, hair, and so on, and that she really needs to ask a female friend, would prevent him from telling the truth.

Another way is to have a prepared scripted answer to such questions, such as telling her that she always looks good to him or she has a beautiful figure/face whatever she does or wears. I would, though, recommend that he does not use the latter unless he truly means it. Sometimes he may have to decide whether total and sometimes brutal honesty is actually worth the pain it causes her and the repercussions it might have on him, which might spoil the whole evening for them both if they are preparing to go out.

The majority of women do not always want the absolute truth, especially about the things they take pride in, no more so than if a man asked if she thought he was a good provider, good in bed or had done a good job papering the front room. If she were to reply by telling him that she thought he had done a rubbish job papering the front room or that he could be a better provider and lover, he would be devastated because he knows he has tried his best and would like that to be enough for her. Most women would like to believe that at least in their partner's eyes they are beautiful and desirable. This is especially the case if a woman has low self-esteem or if feeling good about her appearance is central to her confidence. To take that away from her will only result in feelings of unhappiness and insecurity.

There will without doubt be something about the AS man's partner that he finds desirable or admires. Just giving her some genuine praise or offering a flattering comment can do wonders to boost her self-esteem and make her feel good about herself and, of equal importance, she will feel good about him.

18

My only purpose seems to be to work and earn the money. Is this all I am worth? Why doesn't she appreciate all I do for her (and the family)?

This is the way many men with AS say they feel. Some men state that they feel their partner does not appreciate them, despite all the effort they have made to contribute towards the running of the relationship. The majority of men I see take their responsibilities, of being able to work, finance and supply their family with a comfortable lifestyle, very seriously and they will spend hours upon hours at work or will devote hours of their spare time to doing jobs in the house and garden.

There is no doubt that some men with AS will hold on to very traditional values in their role as husband and father in their family and they often set themselves very high standards and will put in much effort to maintain these standards. So why does it seem that, despite all the efforts they make, their partner is unhappy? Their partner accuses them of not trying to make the relationship work or not putting in any effort to make her and/ or the children happy. This must feel very unfair and unjustified to the man.

To the logical brain of an AS man her accusations and unhappiness will make no sense at all, and will feel totally unjustified. This could result in the AS man having feelings of resentment both towards his partner's lack of appreciation and the fact that his partner seems to voice it constantly. The result is that he will probably withdraw and avoid communication with her; to achieve this he may find he spends even more time at work or being involved in a DIY project. The problem is that rather than alleviating the situation he will find his absence exacerbates it, and the relationship will rapidly become even more strained. He may find his partner becoming even more unhappy and emotionally demanding and, before long, both will find themselves in a never ending loop of discontent and unresolved issues.

The reason for these feelings of discontent is that neither understands what is going on for the other and both will be making assumptions from their own perspective. The AS man needs to feel appreciated for what he brings to the relationship. His contribution will for him be based on what he does and how hard he works for his family. For some men it will be the financial contribution they make and the fact they are able to buy the things the family need. Many of the men will work very hard and be financially generous with their partner; a large proportion of the women I encounter enjoy the benefits of their efforts and take pleasure in a very comfortable lifestyle. However, although these things are important to her (and this importance is often increased if there are children involved), she also needs emotional food to make her feel fulfilled and appreciated by him and will often look to him to be the sole provider of this.

We all need food to survive, not just edible food but also emotional, intellectual and spiritual food. Each partner in an AS/non-AS relationship requires a different type of food from the other. The woman will be looking to him to feed her on an emotional level, and this will be her priority. In very much the same way, the AS man will need intellectual food, but unlike her he will not depend on his partner to be the sole provider of this. The logical, intellectual food the AS man needs can be obtained from different areas in his life. He may gain his intellectual food from the learning he achieves from his special interest or it may be from his profession.

I encounter men from various occupations; top of the list is becoming IT, whereas in the past it was likely to have been engineering. Then there are lecturers, pilots, researchers, policemen, men in the military – a multitude of various occupations. Sometimes these areas of profession have grown out of a special interest and are a major contribution to feeding his intellectual appetite. In addition, his occupation may allow him the time and opportunity to discuss and share his thoughts and ideas with likeminded colleagues. This is how he will get the food he needs in order to thrive.

For the woman it is quite different, as she is seeking emotional food on a level which she believes only he can give her. The emotional food she needs is often quite simple: just a hug, a listening ear, undivided attention, a compliment, a nice word or some flowers with a little love note. These things can appear so simple he probably misses their relevance because it is the type of food he does not require in the same way or dose. Although she is aware that he may have to work long hours or go away with his work, she will miss him and want to know he has missed her. When he comes home from work and does not even think to ask her about her day, she will read this as a sign that he does not care, that he would rather be at work. She will bring this up and to him this will feel as if she is constantly complaining or looking to pick a fight with him. His response will be to distance himself even more.

This will be an opposite response to his partner's, who is likely to seek his attention even more. She will begin to become even more emotionally demanding in her need to be emotionally fed by him. He will struggle to understand what it is he is doing to upset her; he will not be able to work out why she is so unsatisfied; after all, he is doing his best for her and the family.

After a time she will begin to resent his work and the time he spends there. It will become to her like the 'other woman' and she may feel jealous that he puts so much time and effort into work and so little into her or the family. If this happens in a relationship it will put him under a lot of pressure and he will be less willing to spend time with her, as it will not feel safe. He will not be able to make any logical sense of why she complains that he goes to work and yet will happily help him spend his money. There will be no logic in this for him and, just as his partner will not understand why he does not share her need to be intimate and communicate with her, he will not understand the reason for her dissatisfaction with him.

As with the other issues in this book, this can be easily resolved when the couple understand their differences and their very different needs. Often the simple reality is that he will not be able to give her the emotional support in the way she desires it and she will need to find this for herself, whether it is from her close friends or family, or finding a way to spoil herself with pampering, a holiday away with friends or a hobby. If she is able to do this and take a different perspective by looking positively at the hard work and the effort he makes and by seeing his effort as his way of saying 'I love you,' both will benefit. He would also benefit from his partner being more direct and expressive in her emotional needs; for example, if she needs a hug she needs to learn to tell him so.

Likewise, he will need to make the effort to put by one, or maybe two, evenings a week and time at the weekend to give her and the family his presence and attention. This quality time together should be arranged by both of them and maybe both could take it in turns to decide what to do in this time. It could be as extravagant as a day sailing or visiting a stately home, as simple as a take away and a DVD, or maybe as sensual as spending a day in bed together. Once this time together is established then it needs to be almost written in stone so that it becomes a habit and an integral part of the relationship. In this time he must ensure that he takes no phone calls from work, does not go on the internet and does not become preoccupied with his special interest. She, on the other hand, will not be taking calls from friends or family and not doing household tasks in the home or garden.

There is, though, a need here to mention that if there is an understanding of AS between a couple and he still finds that she is making his home life very unhappy (while making heavy financial demands on him), he might question what his role in the relationship is and whether or not he is being financially abused.

19

Why does my partner expect me to come in from work and immediately start discussing the day with her?

This issue is not uncommon and women find it very hard to understand and accept that when their partner with AS comes home from work he is not, like them, bursting to exchange news and experiences and share feelings that have occurred thoughout his day. In an ideal world the woman would like him to walk through the door, immediately seek her out (presuming she is in first), call her name, whisk her up into his arms and tell her how much he has missed her and loves her. The couple would then, while engaging in household chores together, exchange their news and views of their day.

If it is the man who gets in first, then the woman's ideal would be to come home to a warm house, a big hug from him and the smell of cooking in the kitchen. They would share the meal that he had prepared, maybe with a glass of wine, and snuggle up together on the settee. In this time they would again be sharing their news and views on their days.

This is what she would like to happen, not because she is being overdemanding, but because this is how she will get her emotional and intimate needs met. This is what she is, in most cases, prepared and willing to offer him, so without understanding AS she will have no idea why this cannot be reciprocated by him and why the reality of what does happen is probably very different. As in all relationships, there are always two sides and two perspectives. Let's now move over to his perspective.

The AS man is likely to have spent all day working hard, dealing with people, achieving his goals and performing tasks.

Although for many men their jobs can feel taxing and difficult, the problems they are faced with will usually have been logical and his aim will have been to find logical solutions to logical problems. Some of these may not have been straightforward, but nevertheless they are unlikely to have been emotional issues and he will not have spent his day drawing on his feelings, discussing how issues made him feel or having to mindread his colleagues' emotions. In most cases (but not all) he will have been quite securely placed within a logical environment that only required his logical brain to manage and maintain his daily routine.

At the end of the day his logical brain will be full and focused on what he has achieved or not throughout the day, so it will not be easy for him to come home and to detach himself from work and 'empty out' the day's events in order to allow in his partner and family in. Even the journey home will have been spent revisiting and processing events, communications and disputes that may have occurred throughout the day.

He is unlikely to be experiencing that warm feeling of arriving home as he steps over the threshold; in fact quite the opposite, as he will feel he is leaving his safe place of work to enter a very different environment to the one he has left behind. He is entering his partner's environment, one which is unpredictable, emotional and chaotic and, for him, hard work: much harder than the work he has left behind.

He will not be able to make the quick transition from work to home and his logical brain, still full to capacity, will be busy filing and sorting the day's events. He will be unlikely to see the logic in seeking out his partner and greeting her. As one man stated, 'Well, she knows I am home, she will have heard me put the car in the garage. What is the point in telling her something she already knows?'

With this in mind and his focus still on work, he may want to head straight for the computer, in order to check his emails or record a worthwhile idea that occurred to him on the way home. Meanwhile, his partner, desperate for his attention and full of the feelings and issues she wants to share with him, will be making her intentions very obvious. The problem is he will not be ready to hear about her day; he will not be able to offer her emotional support. He is no longer in a safe place; he is no longer in an environment that he feels in control of. Ten minutes spent in the home, with its multiple distractions and emotional demands, leave him feeling more exhausted than ten hours of work.

This is not a choice: it is what makes his brain and hers different; no one is to blame here. Women need to share their experiences and they want to share them with their partner. This is not unreasonable and she is within her rights to want to share her day. In fact it is a compliment, and a sign that she loves her partner and sees him as her friend and confidant. It is not surprising that she feels upset, rejected and irrelevant when he cannot even take the time to say hello and give her a kiss or hug when he comes in.

When two people make a commitment to share their lives together they enter into a contract or a pact. An aspect of this is sharing views, beliefs, opinions and experiences. A partner is often the person that we will turn to first when we have a concern; they are the one we want to spend time with and we value their input in our lives. This would have been one of the reasons that she entered into the committed relationship and she, like him, has a fundamental right to these rudiments in a relationship. Many of the men I encounter appear to offer these rudiments until the point that the relationship becomes established. This established state might be triggered when the couple marry, or live together. Men with AS have been found to completely change their mindset and emphasis at this critical point in the relationship and have been known to completely revert to thinking solo or single.

The woman suddenly finds herself feeling neglected, ignored and no longer particularly relevant in her AS partner's life, except for the basic practicalities she brings to the relationship, such as financially contributing, keeping the house clean, cooking the meals or looking after the children. It will, for her, feel as if the romance died overnight and she suddenly shifted down his order of priorities from number one to maybe number four/five or lower, depending on how full his life is.

Meanwhile (and through no fault of his), he will be blissfully unaware of how she is feeling. He will see that he is fulfilling his role by the fact that he has shown he is committed to her and now seeks on a practical level to maintain the relationship, by working and doing jobs around the house. In the same way he will expect her to fulfil her role on a practical level. The practical side of the relationship though, for her, forms only a part of the liaison and she will feel he has cut off her emotional lifeline. This detachment could cause her to feel insecure and needy.

Strategies can be found to overcome this if both are prepared to make some relatively small changes. For him to make the transition between work and home needs a little time, maybe 30 minutes alone, to shower, go for a run or, for some men, visit the gym on the way home. If she is able to allow him this time in the knowledge that she will get his time and attention at the end of it, then things will improve for both.

If he can remember, as explained for Question 9, that it is the simple things that make her happy, and she is willing to give him the 30 undisturbed minutes of transition time before engaging with her and the family, then it is down to him to make the effort to give her the acknowledgement, attention and time she needs from him.

Rule 7

There is a limit to how much you
can collect and keep in the home!

20

My partner keeps nagging me to get rid of some of my possessions. She does not understand how much stress this causes me. What can I do?

Not all men with AS are obsessive collectors, but those who are appear to do it big time. I have visited houses that were bursting to the seams with prized collections. I have seen rooms packed with DVDs and CDs, magazines, stuffed animals and birds, train sets, models and 'maybe one day I will need it' objects.

Women have been driven to distraction as they have found themselves slowly being forced out of each room by the ever-increasing volume of their AS partner's collection, which seems to grow on a daily basis. Some women have tried to dispense with what they thought were irrelevant objects; they would do this when their partner was out or at work and they have been quite shocked by how quickly he noticed something was missing, and rapidly fished it out of the rubbish bin. For example, Mary described how her partner, John, would never part with his clothes and kept them 'just in case' or as something to wear when he was doing a job. The collection grew and eventually ended up filling the garage. One day she decided to take some old 1970s waistcoats to the local charity shop, feeling sure he would not notice.

John noticed within 24 hours that they were missing and went into a complete meltdown. He felt totally betrayed by her and became paranoid that every time he left the house Mary would get rid of more of his items; his trust in her was completely destroyed. The couple went through a very difficult time after this, despite the fact that Mary had managed to buy them back from the charity shop for him. Mary learnt a very important lesson and did not discard anything of John's again. However, they struggled to hold the relationship together for quite a while.

Finding a balance is very important in relationships, and in cases like the one I have described all balance had been lost. His obsessive need to keep everything was out of control and proportion and it was not fair on her that she should have to tolerate such a vast amount of useless items filling up their house and garage. Neither, though, was it fair that she should discard his items without his knowledge and permission. But it was a very difficult situation for her, knowing that he would never have agreed, no matter how much she tried to explain her feelings.

The home for many women is very important, especially if there are children, and it could well epitomise who she is and how she cares for her family. She may take great pride in how the home looks and feel it represents her and her role in the relationship. This is not dissimilar to how the AS man might feel about the job he does; this will epitomise who he is and also shape a large part of his self-esteem and feeling of worth.

Unlike his work, though, the home is something they share between them and both have to respect each other's role and value within the home. Due to the differing needs that occur within AS/non-AS relationships each will have a need for their own space and, if room allows, maybe an area or room in the house that they can feel is more or less their own territory. In many cases couples have built on a conservatory or workshop to solve this; others may decide on a spare room each, if the space is available. This provides them each with a room that is totally theirs, and they are free to do what they like in it. Where this is an option it seems to work really well for a couple as both feel they can then spend time in a room which represents the environment which they need to thrive.

It is important that rules and boundaries are put into place early on in the relationship and an agreement is reached about how much space each is allowed to dominate in the home. Without this the collecting will become a habit and once a habit has been formed he may find it very difficult, sometimes impossible, to change. They need to come to an agreement on how much space can be dominated by the other. Of course, this varies between couples, but the point is the home belongs to both of them and a balance should be found in how it is divided and organised.

One partner cannot dominate the space over the other. If both are avid collectors, the house is big enough to take it and no one minds living with each other's collections, then there will not be a problem. If, however, the space used up by one partner is reaching a point that it is jeopardising the relationship, a solution needs to be found and some boundaries put in place. This is what being in a relationship is about; it is about being fair and sharing equally. If, though, he feels he still cannot part with his possessions and his collection continues to grow and dominate the space, the couple may find themselves in an impossible situation. If it is impossible to live together in a way that is harmonious and pleases both they will have to decide what the best way forward is.

I have found that living apart can work very well for many couples in AS/non-AS relationships as long as the decision is mutual. When this has been suggested, some men have been fearful that this would mean the end of the relationship, and it is not surprising they feel like that. In reality though, the relationship is more likely to end if they do not live separately and for some couples it is the only way they have found that works. I have found that, for the majority of men with AS, once the move was made and the change adapted to they really came into their own as their stress levels decreased and they began to relish their time alone and the freedom to abide by their own routines and rules.

All options will need to be discussed by the couple and a compromise that will work for them will need to be reached. Obviously, living separately or moving to a larger house is not an option available to all couples. This may be due to financial reasons or not wanting to disrupt the children. What is important is that the arrangement decided on is fair and doable for both parties involved.

21

My wife does not seem to know how to load a dishwasher and yet when I rearrange the contents she gets really mad at me. Why won't she just do things the correct way?

Of course this is not limited to the dishwasher; it may be the order she washes up the dishes, how she stores goods in the cupboards, how she organises the shopping on the conveyor belt or how she packs the shopping into the boot of her car. The list is endless and it will drive the AS man to distraction to observe her doing these things her way and not how he would like it done.

His frustration may build up as time goes on and he may find himself checking and reorganising the way she has placed things so that they fit into a neat, orderly and logical world. If this cycle continues, and she does not adjust her way of ordering things, he may find himself becoming more and more resentful, as he may come to believe she is purposely ignoring his suggestions in order to annoy him. Organising, categorising and ordering may come quite naturally to him; in fact his logical brain may not be able to do things any other way. I am more than used to the client with AS straightening the place mats on the table or getting up to put a picture straight; for some, not doing this would have an effect on their capacity to concentrate on what is being discussed within the counselling room, as they would struggle to ignore the irregularity in the room. Although in many ways there are many benefits of this, it might not seem so to the partner.

The man is likely to have shown his frustration to his partner and made his point about the benefits of structure and order.

However, this might not have made any difference and he will find it difficult to understand why she continues to ignore his well-meant advice. The relevance and importance of ordering and structuring will be quite low on the woman's priority list and there will be many other things that she will feel are more relevant. Her brain will not require objects to form linear patterns and it is less likely her attention will be drawn to these irregularities in her environment.

For example, let us say that the topic in question is how the shopping is placed on the conveyor belt in the supermarket and John and Mary are out shopping together. John had often explained to Mary the usefulness of order and how spending time in the initial stage of taking the goods from the shopping trolley and placing them on the conveyor belt in an appropriate order will save time later. John had already shown Mary this and she will have observed that doing this can indeed make packing the shopping into bags, once their goods have gone through the checkout, much easier. The benefit of taking this time will even extend to when they go home and unpack the shopping, as items for the fridge will be in one bag, freezer goods in another, fruit and vegetables together and finally larder stuff in another bag. This will all appear to him completely logical, very useful and simple to achieve with very little effort.

So imagine how John felt when, after fighting his way back in the crowds to swop a damaged can of tomatoes for an undamaged one, he returned to Mary at the checkout to find she had just thrown everything on to the conveyor belt and the shopping was proceeding through the checkout not in any logical sequence at all. Frozen fish fingers were balanced on top of bottles, heavy cans were squashing the tomatoes and the washing powder was going through with the bread!

The effect of this on John was instant meltdown; he became both angry and agitated. He verbalised his thoughts loudly about Mary's unforgivable deed, which he felt she had done intentionally to annoy him. The girl at the till did not know what to do for the best and Mary felt too shown up for words; she did not even bother to argue or explain. As she felt humiliated and embarrassed she just walked away and left John to pack on his own.

Order and structure are often an important part of the Asperger psyche and I must say AS men are in most cases excellent at it. The AS man is able to achieve order and logic out of absolute chaos if he is given the opportunity. His world is one of linear systems and organised categories; there is no compromise on this and it can be seen as one of the assets he brings to the relationship. It would, however, be more valued and appreciated if he did not make it such an non-negotiable rule that is enforced on the whole family. No one likes to be told what to do or made to feel they are being forced into doing things in a specific way according to someone else.

Most women are excellent at multi-tasking and are better programmed to cope with disorder and chaos. It would be very difficult to bring up children if this was not the case. Children are not predictable, rarely structured and love to make a mess! If a mother decided to attempt to maintain a constant orderly structure in her children's upbringing, she would probably become a complete, worn out, wreck, constantly tidying up after children who were not being allowed to be children, in a house that was for show rather than being a home. For women, time is often more important than order and this was the reason why Mary had just randomly placed the shopping on the conveyor belt at the supermarket. She was on her own and the queue was growing behind her; keeping up to speed and not feeling she was delaying another busy shopper in the queue was more important than maintaining order.

It is a matter of priorities, and both people in the relationship will have their separate and different priority lists. For the AS man it is often structure, the order of things and getting it right that take priority over the time something takes. It is said that if you want a job doing properly then employ someone with AS, but be prepared to wait for it to be completed. He will give doing a perfect job more priority than whether his family have the use of a kitchen or bathroom for weeks. This is when partners will clash: when his need impinges on her and has a direct effect on their quality of time together, and this can appear in all areas of their relationship.

For example, I can recall being told how, when a couple were in the middle of making love, seconds before she reached orgasm, he had to stop what he was doing to get out of bed and straighten a picture on the wall. His partner found this a total passion killer and was shocked that he had given the picture priority over her pleasure and their lovemaking.

In all relationships each partner will be bringing their individual and unique qualities and strengths to the relationship. However, neither has the right to enforce their way of doing things on the rest of the family as this will only result in resentment and a refusal to submit and change. No one has the right to try to change anyone and if a couple find that their way of doing things is very different to each other, they will have to make a choice on how to deal with it. One way is to accept the difference and learn to live with it rather than fight against it and letting it impact negatively on their lives. A better way, though, might be if the person for whom the need is greater can take responsibility for the task and make it their role in the relationship to be accountable for this task. For example, if the issue is about how the shopping is packed or the dishwasher is filled, this can become his role and his responsibility when he is there to take charge of it. This can work well, and I remember one lady telling me how once they reached the conveyor belt, she would go off and enjoy a cappuccino and a blueberry muffin in the café while her partner managed the whole of their weekly shop. Both were content doing what made them happy and they were able to enjoy a far more harmonious relationship.

Rule 8

Do not let a need for order and
structure dominate the whole family.

22

Why does my partner constantly disrupt my plans and routines?

Not all men on the autism spectrum require routine and structure in their lives beyond what would be typically expected in anyone's life. However, for some men the routines and regimes they apply are essential to whether or not they manage to get through the day without a meltdown. Routines, whether functional or non-functional, play a fundamental part in a person's life, as they are normally performed without any conscious thought or planning. For example, getting ready in the morning for work: for some this may involve making a cup of tea, putting the cat out, having a shave, then showering, getting dressed, making breakfast, cleaning teeth and so on. This daily morning routine will be carried out without any conscious thought and probably always in the same order.

There is nothing unusual or objectionable in having fixed routines. However, what can make the difference between a non-AS person and an AS person making use of routine behaviour is how they cope when that routine is disrupted or changed, especially if the disruption is unexpected. Keeping in mind the morning routine above, imagine that the shower breaks down. It would be annoying for anyone, but most would simply adjust accordingly and either forget the shower or have a wash instead and carry on with their day.

But for the person with AS the shower breaking down could cause them to become very stressed and agitated and might well have a profound impact on their whole day. Rather than just change their routine and forget the shower they may try to fix it there and then. This will cause a delay in their schedule and could consequently make them late for work. They may take time trying to find a plumber and then not go into work in order to ensure the plumber can get in and fix it as soon as possible. If the AS person has a partner it is likely that the frustration and agitation the shower breakdown caused will disrupt them and they could find themselves trying to calm things down and rationalise it: 'It is no big deal.' This will not go down very well, as for the AS person it is a very big deal and they may feel let down that their partner is not taking them seriously.

The example of the shower is just one of many that might occur: the fixed routine could be the route driven to and from work, it could be insisting meals are served at a very specific time or that the same foods are served on specific evenings. Some routines are about the order of things and how they are categorised; this could be DVDs, CDs, tools, books and many other things. If this order is disrupted or broken, it can cause stress and anxiety for the AS person. If the need is for items to be ordered in size and there is an item that just does not fit, it could end up being discarded rather than tolerated. This could, for instance, be a book that disrupts the whole symmetrical arrangement of books ordered along the shelf.

Routines do not require conscious thought and are often carried out by rote memory. For the person with AS, whose brain is already working so hard just to manage getting through the day, having a routine and knowing that meals will be at fixed times takes away the unpredictability of life and allows them more free conscious thought to consider other things. Routines are simply performed without any thought or consideration; they are safe and certain, that is until they become disrupted by an unforeseen event or, even worse, the AS man's partner.

To the AS man routines will be high on his priority list and he will have developed a dependence on them. This will be very different to the way his partner will perceive routines; although they will still form part of her daily life they will be flexible and adaptable. Her capacity to be spontaneous and flexible is in part due to being female, unless of course she is affected by obsessive compulsive disorder (OCD) or is also on the spectrum, in which case she may likewise have a need for routine and order.

Presuming, though, this is not the case, a woman's mind is able to switch from one thing to another very quickly and she can easily adapt to a new schedule, however unpredictable it is. Often it is the woman who is the main caregiver for the children, and children do not come with routines and order: they can be happy one minute and disruptive the next. When they need the toilet, everything will stop in order to get them there in time. A mother's brain will easily bend and adjust to her children's needs without any need to have a scripted plan.

Such a woman, living with a man with AS who has a need for strict and inflexible routines, might in the initial stage of the relationship be quite enamoured by his ability to organise and structure. She may have tried hard to fit in with him; she will, however, be presuming that when circumstances change then so will he and that he will adapt to new and different situations.

She may expect this to happen when they move in together. It may come as a shock to her when she discovers that his routines are written in stone and he will not compromise them on any level. Some will engineer their lives to fit in with this and make a lot of effort to have meals on the table at specific times, and will do things in the order he requires. However, many women in this situation report feeling very controlled and unhappy; they feel stripped of their spontaneity as they are no longer allowed freedom of choice.

In time these women may rebel, unwilling to allow their AS partner to have so much control over them and, possibly, their children. Alternatively, the woman may have refused to fit in from the very start of the relationship, because her identity is strong enough not to allow it to be controlled or moulded. Either way, it is unlikely that she will understand the relevance and importance of routines and why he needs them. I do not feel he should expect her or the rest of the family to adapt to his routines, as no one has the right to try to change another person. However, as long as his routines can be organised to not affect her or the family he should be allowed to adhere to them and this need should be respected by her.

If, though, an understanding of Asperger syndrome has not evolved between the couple it is unlikely she will comprehend why routines are so important to him. For example, every Saturday morning John followed a very specific routine and knew exactly what he was going to do and achieve in that time. He always met up with a close friend in Waterstones for an espresso coffee at 10.00 am; after this he would walk down to the gym and spend an hour working out. John would then go to his favourite café and enjoy a bacon sandwich with a hot mug of coffee. Nothing particularly special, but for him it was his time to unwind after a busy week at work and do the things he enjoyed and totally deserved.

So when Mary, his partner, asked him to call in at her mother's on his way to town and tune in her new digital television for her, he was completely thrown and felt that all his plans were being sabotaged. John did not want to run the risk of a possible confrontation by saying no to Mary, but was not able to hide his frustration and annoyance at being asked to do something that to him was not urgent and would completely disrupt his morning.

Mary quickly picked up on his negative reaction and accused him of being selfish and not caring about her elderly mother who was disabled and living alone. Things soon went from bad to worse and Mary ended up shouting at him that she would get someone else to do it, because he obviously put his own needs first over those of other people in his life. To this John had said 'good' and walked out. By now he was already late and could not get himself back on track.

In the case described John had unintentionally given Mary the message that meeting his friend, going to the gym and having lunch out were more important than the needs of his mother in law. To Mary this was made very clear by his actions, but this was not the case, as he did care about his mother in law and would have been quite willing to go round and tune in the television as long as it did not conflict with his plans. To John there was no urgency attached to tuning in the television and he felt he could have fitted this in on his way home.

For some men with AS to live their lives without routine and structure would be impossible and is not a choice. Of course, this is not an issue to anyone if the man lives alone, but if he is in a relationship then how his routines impact on his partner, their family and quality time together will need to be taken into consideration.

The ideal way to prevent routines dominating a relationship would be not to allow routines that could impinge on couple time to develop in the first place. This, though, would require that the couple had an awareness and understanding of AS from the beginning. Unfortunately this is rarely the case. Therefore the man will need to make the effort to limit his dependence on routines in his life and work on a way that they can be adapted or monitored to fit in with the relationship. This might mean keeping fixed routines to weekly working days only and ensuring that the weekend is routine free and more flexible. Through the working week there may need to be an adherence to fixed times and having a morning routine that is regulated by time and order may play an important role in ensuring he arrives at work on time. However, at the weekend or on non-workdays the couple could arrange not to allow such strict routines to develop. If plans are being made for the weekends and holidays then they need to be made together to ensure that both partners' needs are being met and the couple can have quality time together. For instance, using the example of John and Mary, it could be arranged that John's mornings belonged to him and the afternoons would be dedicated to doing things together.

If both in the relationship are aware of AS and have an understanding of it, compromise can be reached, as long as both remember to consider the other's needs and differences. He needs to be aware that her world is flexible and not built out of a need for intransigent structure and repetitive regimes. Her needs are about maintaining the family's infrastructure and their need to connect and remain emotionally healthy.

She, however, will need to take into account her partner's need for inflexible and repetitive routines as they will free up his brain to allow him the extra time and energy to offer to other needs, such as those of his partner and family. Having routines in his life will be his way of automatically structuring his day so he will not require the extra thought to restructure spontaneously and will give him the added bonus of helping to prevent overload.

Both in the relationship will benefit from having structure and routines in their lives. However, it is again about moderation, balance and ensuring that one's own needs are not having a destructive effect on the rest of the family.

23

Why does my partner have to announce everything we do on Facebook? Surely I am entitled to some privacy in my life?

The words 'Facebook' and 'Twitter' seem to be on everyone's tongue of late. Facebook and Twitter appear to serve different purposes for different people. For example, women are more inclined to use them to share information with others whereas men, and especially men with AS, are more inclined to use them to collect information about others. It is a way of communicating news as quickly as possible to as many people as possible and for some it is becoming a major focus and pastime in their lives, conversation and thoughts. Facebook members have a window into others' lives and can, if not controlled and monitored, make very public some issues that might have been better kept private.

It is the nature of many men with AS to be very private about their personal lives and few will go into work on a Monday morning eager to regurgitate the entire weekend's events and disclose everything his family and he did, ate and shared together. The private world of AS men is very precious to them and needs to be respected by those who share their lives. Unfortunately, though, for some men, it feels as though it is not always the case and they find their lives being made very public. In the majority of cases these disclosures by a female partner are not made out of spite or to hurt them. This is again an example of how each partner operates differently.

The world of women operates in a very different way to that of men. The majority of women like to share, disclose, discuss and gossip about events and news that have impacted on their lives and others'. One of the reasons for this is that they enjoy being able to discuss their feelings and to share and compare those feelings with others. Sharing is part of their world, it reduces their stress level and helps them keep their feelings balanced and in control.

Disclosing, discussing and sharing emotions is an integral part of how women thrive and survive. For example, a man discovered that his partner had announced on Facebook that he had not managed to complete the London marathon, and this information filtered through to his work colleagues. He felt this was a betrayal by her and that she had done it to humiliate him. Of course, she did not post the news to make him look as though he had failed. She did not do it to spite him or to break his trust in her as a confidant. Her reasons were quite simple and straightforward (remember – women are not rocket science!). His wife felt sorry for her husband and knew how devastated he was for not having completed the marathon. She knew how hard he had exercised for this; every Sunday he had got up at 6.00 am to go out running; she knew how he so wanted that coveted precious medal to hang up in his studio. She felt pained over his pain, she was being empathetic and had felt quite down and sad for him.

As a very caring and empathetic woman she wanted to share her feelings with other women. She needed an emotional response and support from others to help console her and make her feel better. Women need to talk and share their feelings. They do not have the same capacity as many men with AS to put feelings into a box and analyse them logically while viewing emotional situations from a practical and objective viewpoint. This is not possible for them, and if she was of this type and character he would probably not have been attracted to her in the first place.

Men with AS are attracted to highly emotional, nurturing and caring women. About 98 per cent of the non-AS women I see who have partners with AS work in the caring profession and many of the 2 per cent that do not can be found to be somewhere on the autistic spectrum too. This is not simply coincidence, and an AS man who finds a woman with the qualities of high emotional empathetic thought and then presumes she will not have the need to share her feelings is going to be disappointed.

It is important that the couple discuss in advance what is OK and not OK to disclose about the other. For example, the man who did not complete the marathon would have been wise to have told his partner that besides, say, her best friend or mother, he would rather she kept this information to herself as he did not want people to know. If she understands AS she will understand that the reason he does not want to disclose private information such as this will not be to hide the fact he failed to complete the marathon, but because of the fear of finding himself in the awkward position of having to discuss *his feelings* about not completing it.

Men with AS rarely disclose situations and events in their lives which provoke feelings or would be likely to result in them having to discuss their feelings openly. There are examples of men with AS suffering the death of a loved one or discovering they have an illness themselves and not sharing this information with close family and friends. Non-disclosure, though, does not come as a surprise when looking at the nature of AS, which can make it very difficult to discuss emotions with others.

Disclosing his feelings would not make a man with AS feel any better, as logically it would not change the situation or improve it in any way. Unless the person disclosed to was a doctor or professional who could offer some advice or medication there would seem no point. It can feel far better and far safer for the AS man to just pop it in a box in his mind and focus on the things that do make him feel better and more fulfilled.

His partner will need to understand that lack of disclosure by him about issues that could trigger an emotional response from others is not his way of playing the victim or trying to adopt a stiff upper lip. It is about the way his mind works and copes with emotional events in his life. He does not have the same needs as her and both need an acceptance here of each other's different worlds.

24

She constantly accuses me of not listening to her and forgetting what she has told me. Is she making this up to put me down or do I really have memory problems?

In Allan and Barbara Pease's book, appropriately called *Why Men Don't Listen and Women Can't Read Maps* (2001), it is suggested that to get a man to listen, a woman would be well advised to give him prior warning and an agenda. Much of the advice given in this entertaining book could be applied here as it is likely to be the case that it is not so much that the AS man does not listen to what his partner says, as about how and when she delivers the message to him.

In our busy lives it is often the case that a couple may just get snatches of time together and these are normally during the busiest and most chaotic times of the day, such as breakfast, the children's bathtime or when one partner is preoccupied. In this case let's presume it is breakfast time and Mary is giving the children their breakfast when John enters the kitchen diner. He joins them at the table and the conversation (or monologue) may go something like this:

> **Mary** 'I spoke to Mum last night – she sends you her love by the way – oh, I have such a headache – anyway we need to book the tickets for the pantomime. Oh, hang on a minute, the toast is burning! Well, I was wondering if you had time – Johnny don't you dare start playing up again, you have just gone and got Weetabix all over your sleeve! Oh, I have such a headache! What was I saying? Oh yes – can you

book seats as close to the front as possible and collect them on your way home?'

John, meanwhile, had heard little of what Mary said as he was far too distracted by the fact little Johnny was dabbing the sleeve of his clean pullover in his Weetabix. The obvious consequence of this was that when he returned home and Mary asked if he had collected the tickets, he had absolutely no memory of any such request made by her or any conversation remotely connected to the theatre. Consequently, he absolutely denied that she had even told him about the theatre or made such a request. John's belief was that Mary had not told him and that it was she who had got this wrong. He felt that he was being blamed and attacked for something that he was not guilty of and was not his fault.

It was understandable that John felt like this and not surprising that he felt he was being picked on. He had absolutely no memory of her asking him to get the tickets and the reason for this was that there were too many distractions at the time when she told him.

How men and women interact and their communication abilities can appear to be quite different from each other. A woman's communication style may include more emotional and descriptive words, whereas a man's communication style may tend to be more logical and direct. These variances could be due to the differences between the male and female brain types. Simon Baron-Cohen presents much evidence to support his description of the female brain as the empathiser and the male brain as the systemiser (Baron-Cohen 2003). Baron-Cohen has described men on the autistic spectrum as having an extreme form of the male brain (Baron-Cohen 2003).

My research (Aston 2001, p.29) found that the female partners of men with AS tended to be very intuitive, empathetic and caring women – this could suggest that they were at the other end of the spectrum and have a very highly tuned female brain. Baron-Cohen also suggests that women such as these could be described as having an extreme form of the female brain. He gives the example of the endlessly patient psychotherapist (Baron-Cohen 2003, p.173) and it is not surprising to discover that the majority of female partners I see work in the caring professions.

This difference in brain types between a couple will not only affect how each perceives the world and interacts and relates to others, it will also exaggerate the differences in their style of communicating. Many of the men I see are inclined to get straight to the point very quickly, use few adjectives and keep their communication quite literal and abbreviated, whereas the women will use more words and more adjectives, and describe how something made them feel in much more detail.

Most women are able to multi-task with more ease than men and this is also evident in their communication style, as they are often experts at being able to think about and consider many topics at the same time and therefore often include many messages in one sentence. They do not always make it clear which parts of the messages should be given priority by the listener.

Women may rely on their non-verbal body language to compensate for this ambiguity in their communication and the relevant importance of each topic in their message will thus be made clear to the listener. Unfortunately, a partner with AS will not be able to read her body language accurately and may miss altogether the importance or relevance of the message she is delivering.

Women (or those with a stronger female brain) appear to have a better capacity to sieve through communication and decipher what is relevant and what is not than men (or those with a stronger male brain) and would have quickly realised that the relevant part of Mary's communication was to pick up the theatre tickets.

Due to the fact that John is both male and has Asperger syndrome he was not able to do this. It is likely that the whole paragraph would have sounded the same, with no indication of what was relevant, whether it was the toast burning or picking up the tickets for the theatre. John would have stopped hearing anything Mary was saying the second his attention was distracted by the fact that his young son's sleeve was being dabbed in his

Weetabix! His partner would not have known that he had not heard. He was stood in front of her and she assumed that as he did not query her request he must have heard and understood. Once again, both are caught up in a no-blame situation.

There are, though, other times when a man with AS may not be able to recall conversations accurately; this is during the time he is in meltdown. When a person with Asperger syndrome goes into meltdown or overloads it is often a consequence of their logical brain no longer being able to keep up to speed with the high input of information it is trying to process. Too many sensory stimuli will cause the brain to become completely overloaded and overwhelmed with information. If the communication is about feelings or is becoming emotional, he will reach a point of meltdown much faster – the reason this happens is because the logical part of his brain is trying to translate and process information that is completely illogical and has no order or structure to it.

Meltdown is also called 'overload' and it is exactly that for the person experiencing this; their brain is absolutely overloaded and there is no room left for any more information to be processed. Consequently much information will not make it to long-term memory and will be totally lost in translation. I hear accounts from the majority of couples I see that there is an issue with the memory of conversations and how they are recorded and perceived. Many couples find that when they try to talk over a precarious or sensitive issue that has occurred between them, their memory of the incident is very different. The result is that the couple find themselves getting stuck on the words they are using to describe the event as the other partner is correcting them for not being accurate, while voicing a very different story altogether. The consequence is that the couple end up falling out over the memory of the situation and are unable to resolve the meaning behind the issue as they don't recall it in the same way.

The reason for this is not that the AS man is trying to change or avoid the truth; it is simply that when he was in overload some information will have been lost or disjointed and the memory will not be there to recall. It is once again a situation when no one is to blame and there is no right or wrong.

It is important for the AS man to be aware that he may miss important messages that his partner is giving him and for them to agree together that it would be wise for her to write all important messages down for him. This way he can use the written note as a reminder or, even better, she could put it on a Post-it note and stick it to his dashboard or some very obvious place, so he cannot forget: a simple solution, which could save much anguish and stress for both of them and avoid future falling outs over something that is the not the fault of either.

If, though, we are talking about information not being processed due to him being in overload, then it will not be possible to write things down. So unless the couple are able to record every time they have a dispute there will be no way of having factual reminders of what happened. Memory recall of such situations will be entirely dependent on each person's memory banks and what is stored there.

The AS partner will need to be aware that in the case of overload his memory may not have all the information of what was said and done stored away. Therefore if he finds she is bringing up something he said or did of which he has no memory, it will not always be the case that she is making it up, exaggerating or being overcritical. The best way forward when this happens would be for him to say that, although he cannot remember the incident, he apologises for how this has made her feel and reassures her that it would not have been his intention to hurt her, but that it was simply a consequence of heated feelings at the time.

On her part she will need to make allowances for how hard her partner's brain is working in order to accommodate their differences in communication. She will need to appreciate and respect that his brain is processing information differently to hers and he is not blessed with being able to make use of multiple routes in his brain. She will need to write important messages down as reminders and choose the timing carefully for delivering her relevant messages.

There will be no use trying to hold a constructive conversation with him if there are too many distractions going on, as he will not hear her and he will have no memory of the message she gave him. She will also need to accept that after a falling out or meltdown he may not remember things the same way she does. Most important is that if her partner apologises she must accept this and respect his apology even if he professes not to have any memory of the situation. If he cannot remember it there will be little to be achieved by revisiting it and flogging the memory to death as she will not trigger his memory of it.

25

My partner complains that I spend too much time on the internet and not enough time with her, and yet when I try to spend time with her she just wants to watch soaps! I think she is being unreasonable. Is she?

The answer to this question is yes and no. Let us deal with the yes first. The internet, or the time the AS man may spend on the internet, is becoming quite a problem in some of the relationships I encounter. In fact it is an issue which is escalating as computers and the internet offer the man with AS the perfect source of information and an excellent medium for him to dedicate his time to. The problem is that the internet has a very addictive appeal that quickly takes hold and can easily escalate out of all proportion.

Research has revealed that engineering appeared to contain a proportionally higher percentage of the AS population than other occupations (Baron-Cohen *et al.* 1997). My own observations suggest that engineering is rapidly being replaced by occupations within IT, and this can be everything from programming or web design to repairing computers or selling computer software. Not all, but the majority of, people with AS appear to have a natural aptitude for IT and people with AS are responsible for many of our technical advances in this area.

IT, like mathematics, is about logical thinking; it is based on numbers and systems, and requires an intense focus and the ability to see detail while being able to work in a strategic manner. Some men with AS have used IT analogies to explain how they feel their own brain works. They may describe seeing life in a series of systems and compartments, their thinking is logical and literal, and it does not get distracted by emotions or hypothetical thought, very much like the way a computer operates.

The internet has much to offer the AS male, especially information, which can be as necessary to him to thrive as emotions are to his female partner. The Asperger brain can be described as a sponge that will soak up information, seeking it out and devouring it as though it were food. The problem is that the internet can become addictive and quickly take over his life, leaving little time for anything else. He may find he will be so absorbed with the world of cyberspace that he will lose all sense of time and of what is going on around him, including how lonely and neglected his partner is feeling.

His partner will be feeling like an internet widow; she may already be trying to cope with and tolerate his long hours at work and now she finds that when he comes home he disappears in front of the computer and she is lucky if he stops to eat or come to bed at the same time as her. A relationship cannot survive such neglect for long and she will find herself reaching such a point of desperation and loneliness that she will begin to question exactly what she is getting out of the relationship.

She has a right to quality time with her partner and his time on the computer will have to be capped or controlled before the habit becomes too fixed, otherwise it will be very difficult for him to change and almost impossible to break the habit. The man has to decide what he wants most, to live on the internet or with her, because he cannot lead a solitary life *and* have a relationship. It is unworkable and a balance will have to be found if he does not want to find himself alone.

Finding a balance between autonomy and intimacy is important in any relationship and if a couple want a healthy relationship then it is critical that this balance is achieved. The AS man will be fighting for his autonomy, while she will be fighting for intimacy. The more the couple fight the deeper each will dig their trenches and stake their stronghold, refusing to move an inch.

One AS man once said to me that compromise was a meal eaten cold and that it would mean dissatisfaction and self-deprivation on the part of the one who has made the sacrifice. I say compromise is a meal eaten warm, not so hot that it burns and not so cold that it is unpalatable, but warm. This, however, will only come about if both partners feel their forfeit is equal and their gain is even. If the changes and compromises are not balanced then it will leave one partner feeling resentful and hard done by.

If the relationship is to survive it will require that he limits the time he spends on the internet and this is something that should be negotiated between them. Once this is decided then it needs to be decided what that time will be replaced with. This is where the 'yes' to the initial question comes into place: if she expects him to give up his time simply to participate in a pastime that only she enjoys, then for him it will indeed feel like a meal eaten cold!

Watching soaps for her can have a much stronger appeal than it will for him. For some women the time they spend watching soaps will offer them the same value and quality time as his being on the internet. The internet provides stimulating logical intellectual food for him and soaps can provide stimulating, unpredictable, exciting and emotional food for her. Both have a right to seek comfort in their chosen area but neither should expect the other to share or participate in their individual interest.

If a man is spending too much time on the internet and not enough time with his partner (and he will soon know this is the case because she will have told him many times), he will need to make changes to his schedule if he wants the relationship to remain harmonious. This will require that he limits the time he spends on the internet and replace it with time spent with his partner.

However, if he is willing to do this it is only fair that she makes the same compromise. If the time together conflicts with the television programmes she enjoys then she will need to record them, and watch them while he is having his time on the internet. The time the couple agree to share needs to be quality time and time spent doing things they both find enjoyable, for example, sharing a DVD that they wish to watch together, playing games, conversing, enjoying a meal together or having sex.

26

My partner discovered I had been looking at porn on the internet. She is now threatening me with divorce. Why is she taking it so out of proportion?

Easy access to internet porn is becoming an increasing problem within relationships today and is an area that can be particularly devastating in any relationship. However, within the AS/non-AS relationship the obsessive nature and communication difficulties affecting the AS man can exacerbate the consequences of internet porn, and unless it is nipped in the bud early on it can devastate a relationship and in many cases bring it to the brink of a divorce.

Men, more than women, appear to be stimulated by the visual aspects of the opposite sex and will seek out this visual stimulation. It is often physical attraction to a particular female that triggers his desire to get to know her more. Throughout history men have been stimulated by observing female nudity and beauty, and a study by Hamann *et al.* (2004) using functional magnetic resonance imaging (fMRI) found that when viewing identical sexual stimuli both the brain areas known as the hypothalamus and amygdala were more highly activated in men than women. Men with AS are no exception to this and, as many are already excellent visualizers, their need of visual stimuli is often heightened and they can be highly stimulated by using voyeurism.

Before the internet, resources to indulge in sexual fantasies of voyeurism were limited to top shelf magazines or visiting strip shows. Access to such spectacles was limited though and this restriction acted as a boundary to married men who might want to indulge in this erotic area. Magazines could easily be found by their partner and often were, and for men to find time to visit a strip show and not to arouse the suspicions of their partner could have been difficult. The attitude towards porn in the past was often one of 'men will be men', as it was less threatening due to censorship and limited access. It would not have been uncommon for a man to have a calendar displaying an array of large-bosomed women hanging on his office wall; it is also unlikely that this would have caused major objections from their partner. Their partners were more than aware of this and saw it as a 'naughty boy thing' rather than feeling threatened by it.

Today, however, the situation is quite different and access to porn, including hard porn, has never been easier and hence more tempting. At the click of a button a person can have access to a multitude of visual erotic displays and with payment he can choose exactly what type of women he wishes to see. With some of the men I have worked with this journey into heavy and obsessive porn often begins with an almost innocent curiosity. Unfortunately, sites are adept at drawing them in and before they know they are caught up in a web of obsessive fantasy.

Internet porn can hold a very strong appeal for men in general; however, for men with AS it is more likely to become obsessive and can offer a safer option than the real thing as it does not require any emotional effort. Cybersex is cold, clinical, does not require communication or emotions, provides visual stimulation and enhances masturbation.

If the discovery of internet porn occurs at the same time that things are not working out sexually with a couple and he is feeling rejected or unwanted by her, then internet porn can quickly become a sexual substitute and eventually replace sexual activity between the couple. Before long he may soon find himself taking solace this way and it is unlikely he will feel any guilt about this: he will not perceive it as being unfaithful because logically, to him, he has not engaged in a physical sexual encounter with another woman. He has not touched, kissed, caressed or had sex with anyone besides his partner, so when she discovers his secret pastime he is not likely to perceive it as a problem or understand why she views it as a betrayal of her trust. He, on the other hand, might argue that she has betrayed him by checking his activities on the internet; however, it is often the case that she was simply following up her gut feeling that something was amiss.

Men with AS, as with any man, are capable of lying, but having AS will impair their ability to lie convincingly. Women, on the other hand, come equipped with a strong sense of intuition and can often tell when something is amiss. In her book *Women Who Stay with Men Who Stray*, Debbie Then reported that 90 per cent of women who suspected their partners were having an affair were right. This strong intuition or sixth sense is an ability that men with AS do not come equipped with, so they will not be aware of the signs and signals their partners are reading in them.

When the woman eventually discovers the porn her partner has been using, he may be quite taken back by the strength of her response. She is likely to feel hurt and cheated and her reaction could be one of extreme anger or sorrow. Whichever way she reacts he will see it as an overreaction and unfortunately may not show the appropriate remorse for the situation, which would help ease her insecurities.

This is where Asperger syndrome comes into the equation, as a non-AS man, if caught indulging in internet porn, is likely to show deep remorse at being discovered and apologise for the pain and hurt this has caused her. He would explain his reasons, describe to her how sexually lonely and rejected he had been feeling, and might suggest they go to counselling to sort it out and try to rebuild the sexual side of their relationship. He would also reassure her that this did not mean he would be unfaithful and she was the only one he wanted to be sexual with. This would have given her the acknowledgement and attention she needed to help her work it through and would be the first step to regaining her trust in him.

Unfortunately, the man with AS will struggle to see things from her perspective, so rather than make her feelings the priority he will be busy defending himself, justifying to her why he did it and projecting the blame on to her. He will not be acknowledging that her reaction is based on his behaviour and he needs to be making her feel better. This lack of empathy and concern for her feelings will quickly cause the situation to escalate because she will not feel convinced that he has any intention of changing his behaviour and not continuing to seek out porn. She will correctly rationalise that if he does not believe that he has done anything wrong then why would he change the behaviour? Often these suspicions prove to be right and the obsession will continue, and her trust will eventually be lost altogether as she realises he is not hearing her anguish and taking her seriously.

Once this stage is reached it is for the woman no longer just about the porn; it is now about trust, and this will cause more damage to the relationship than the actual porn element. Everything is about balance and if she feels he is looking at porn in preference to her, if she feels he is willing to put the whole relationship in jeopardy to fulfil his sexual needs, then she may decide to end the relationship.

If the man does not want to lose his partner's trust or risk the relationship breaking down altogether then he will need to take his partner's feelings seriously and accept what she is saying. Although the AS man might not understand why she is reacting in this way, and he might not feel he has done anything wrong, if he does not end the behaviour it is very likely that the relationship will become a very volatile and unhappy one.

Everyone has different opinions on what constitutes being unfaithful and if a man's partner is refusing to have sex with him then he may rationalise that his behaviour is justified. However, at the end of the day, she is the woman he chose to be with. If her view is that he is being unfaithful to her by being aroused by looking at other women on the internet then her views need to be respected.

Just like her, though, the man also has rights and if he is willing to break the habit of internet porn and yet is still being denied any physical contact with his partner then they should both consider seeing a therapist to help them work through this together. If his partner still refuses to work at this or offer him any affection, then he has two choices: either to inform her that he will need to revert to masturbation as a way of satisfying his sexual needs or to consider if the relationship gives him enough to compensate for leading a celibate lifestyle. Lovemaking is a very important part of the relationship and is what makes the difference between two people just being close friends and being lovers.

27

I feel like I am living with Jekyll and Hyde. For two weeks out of every month my partner seems to have a personality change. She blames it on PMT. Is it really that bad?

In some case the answer to this is yes. Premenstrual tension can cause absolute havoc with a woman's hormones, resulting in drastic changes to her emotions, physical wellbeing and sexual desires. If a man has a partner affected by PMT then he needs to be aware of a few facts and develop some strategies to help both of them survive its effect. First of all, though, it is important for him to understand just what it is and why its effect is so powerful.

The average female menstrual cycle is 28 days; this can, however, vary from 24 to 35 days. The menstrual cycle can be divided into four phases, each serving a different purpose. The first phase is called the proliferative phase and its purpose is to prepare the womb for the possibility that a baby will be conceived. This phase begins two days after a woman begins to menstruate. In this time there is an increase in the hormone oestrogen which will reach its peak at the time of ovulation, which is normally on the 14th day after the start of menstruation. The ovulation phase will last only 24 to 36 hours and then the secretory phase begins and the corpus luteum will secrete the hormone progesterone as well as oestrogen. This will cause the lining of the womb to thicken in preparation for the arrival of a fertilised egg. The secretory phase will last around 10 to 12 days and if the egg has not been fertilised the corpus luteum will cease to produce either hormone and the womb will shed its lining as it enters the menstruation phase.

This describes the biology of what happens; now I will describe the possible emotional effects it may have on the female partner and the relationship. The first phase and up until ovulation is the good phase; this is due to the hormone oestrogen being released. At this time the woman will be relatively calm and in control and, as the days go on towards ovulation, she could be quite affectionate and sensual. When ovulation is reached the woman may become quite sexual and attentive; if you make love at this time you may notice an increased wetness and openness in her vagina. Some women instinctively know when this time is and will affectionately call it 'baby making time'; they are at their peak sexually and can be easy to arouse and satisfy.

The third stage, the secretary phase, is often when the problems start and some men are really taken aback by the change they see in their partner. She may cease to be sexual, may be irritable, easy to anger, emotional and appear quite discontented with the relationship. This can take some men unawares and they may find it really difficult to make sense of such inconsistency. This will change again when her period begins and although she may feel much physical discomfort with stomach cramps and heavy periods, her frame of mind will be less volatile and unpredictable.

For a man with AS this inconsistency in his partner can be hard to understand or live with, and many withdraw and may find they spend longer at work in the second two weeks of her cycle. There are different remedies a woman can try to alleviate the effects of PMT and it is often a matter of trial and error.

As well as it being a difficult time for him, it is likewise a hard time for the woman, as she will be aware of her mood swings, but not feel able to do anything to change them and their effect on her and how she feels. As well as the emotional effects, she will be feeling less attractive and bloated, have an increased appetite which will make her feel even less attractive, and generally not feel on top form. She will certainly not like how she feels in the second two weeks of her cycle, and it is for her to find ways to not let her emotions project themselves onto her partner: she will need to seek out ways to dampen the symptoms she is experiencing.

What the AS man can do is, first of all, keep a diary so he knows exactly what phase his partner is in. It will be better for him to be aware and able to predict both the good phase and the not so good phase. If he can help more with the children or around the house in the second stage then this will alleviate the pressure she feels under. When things are good between them, they should discuss the issue of PMT. He can let her know he is aware and understands this is difficult for her and ask her what it is she would like him to do at this time. She may be happy for him to keep his distance at this time or she may ask for his support.

It is important, though, that the AS man does not become a two week a month scapegoat. Her feeling of irritability will not be her fault as she will have no control over this, neither though is it his fault and he should not have to be the one her anger is taken out on.

It is also necessary to point out here that the AS man must be careful he does not use PMT as an explanation for all his partner's emotions, as although PMT will exacerbate her emotions it will not be the primary cause of her ups and downs and it is important for the AS man always to check out first what is affecting his partner rather than assuming that PMT is the reason.

If PMT is an issue between a couple then they will need to try talking about this together when things are good between them and if a resolution cannot be reached and the female partner will not seek remedies to help her, then maybe professional help is needed.

28

Why does she get angry and upset if I don't call or text her at least once a day?

I have talked about the reasons why most women will need to be told more than once that their partner loves them and explained that this is how they find their emotional food from him. The woman will also find that confirmation that he is thinking about her when he is absent gives her reassurance. This confirmation can be sent in a text, email or a telephone call. It can be brief – just a message saying that he is thinking about her and is looking forward to seeing her later will often suffice.

Once again this is something that is quite simple to achieve and certainly not time consuming. However, the reason his partner needs this regular confirmation from him is unlikely to make any sense to the AS man whatsoever, and when something makes no sense to someone it is doubtful that it will be remembered.

For many men with AS, trying to figure out what is going on in their partner's brains is very difficult, and to try to figure out what is going on in their emotions and come up with the right answer is almost impossible. Because of this her actions or requests may be interpreted wrongly, especially if he finds he is being regularly reprimanded for not contacting her. However, the reason that she will be upset or express feelings of being unloved or let down by him is because she, like him, will not be able to make any sense of why it seems that when he walks out of the door she ceases to be of any relevance to him or enter into his thoughts.

One of the reasons this issue may feel so hard to figure out for both of them is because they are so very different in how they think and process information. Each may come to the relationship with a very different set of priorities and will almost certainly have a different set of needs.

The woman looks to her partner to feed her emotionally, to make her feel special, to let her know he is thinking about her. Unfortunately for her, the man with AS will often have other things on his mind and will be too preoccupied to allow thoughts of his partner to come into his mind. AS men are gifted with the ability to focus, and while they are focusing they will be avoiding any form of distraction. They may find it difficult to multi-task and just to switch from one role to another will take time. While the AS man is at work, his whole focus will be on the job; often a perfectionist, he will be seeking to get things right. He will avoid at all costs the possibility of getting things wrong, especially if he has a fear of what others will think of him.

Meanwhile she may be at home, keeping things going, rushing around with the kids and often looking forward to when he comes home so she can share her day with him, or she may be at work and, like him, busy getting on with her day's pressures and work. Unlike him, though, whether at home or at work she will still wonder what he is doing, and whether he is thinking about her too. Thoughts of whether he is also looking forward to seeing her will enter her head; she may send him a text to say hello and ask how he is doing. One of her purposes behind this will be because she wants a reply and she will often find herself waiting for a text back from him – and waiting and waiting.

Eventually she will become concerned something is wrong and she may call him, despite knowing she should not call when he is at work. The response she seeks is confirmation that he is OK, for him to appreciate that she has been concerned about him and for him to explain why he did not answer her text. These responses are unlikely to occur, especially if he is busy and preoccupied when she calls. Understandably his response to her could be quite short and abrupt, such as 'Of course I am all right, what on earth are you concerned about?' She will now feel unloved and unappreciated and not understand why he cannot be as pleased to talk to her as she is to him. Consequently an argument has probably already started before he even gets home.

The AS man finds emotionality very difficult to understand as it is quite alien to his world and nature. He may rationalise that he knows he loves his partner, and question why the fact he is at work is not proof enough of his love and commitment. So why does he need to keep reassuring her when nothing has changed? He loved her when he left for work; where is the logic in her need for him to call or text to tell her again what she already knows? Why does she expect him to be thinking about her when he is busy?

He does not have the time to think about her at work and, after all, logically what good would it do if he did? In fact it would probably be detrimental to him and others if he was not concentrating on the job in hand, as he could easily make a mistake. I must say here that for some of the men I work with this is very true and could result in the cost of someone's life as many do highly responsible jobs, such as that of a pilot or an anaesthetist.

Unfortunately, for AS men the two things in life which cannot be made logical are love and emotions. They will struggle hard to make sense of their partner's emotional needs, why she is reliant on their continued affirmation of their love and why this seems to be paramount to her wellbeing and self-esteem. When I am working with couples this is a very significant obstacle for both to overcome in the relationship if it is going to progress and work successfully.

A man with AS cannot be expected to understand this need for affirmation his partner has. It will be impossible for him to truly make sense of a need so outside his realm of understanding, and one that will also appear to him as both illogical and irrational. I do not seek in my work to offer him an understanding of her need, as what is important and within his capacity is to accept that she has different needs from him and that he will need to find ways to satisfy them when he can. If it is something as simple as sending her a text or giving a call now and then, the effort will be worth it and he will be arriving home to a happier and more contented partner.

However, it is just as important that she does not have expectations of him that are unrealistic. If she expects him to flood her with texts, emails or calls then I am afraid she will be disappointed. Some women will argue that he did these things when they first met so why can't he now? I have to remind them that in the beginning they were the focus of his attention, his special interest, so, yes, they were constantly on his mind. However, that would have changed for him when they became a couple and he was able to return to his comfortable zone, which is often his work or hobbies. When that happened she ceased to be the focus of his attention; he still loved and cared for her, but the way he showed it had changed as he adapted to a lifestyle he could comfortably manage and maintain.

Both will have to accept that the other is not withholding love from them and that if he or she gets it wrong or does not remember to reassure the other, then it must not be taken as a personal attack or a sign that love has died. Rather, it is just a reminder of difference between them that, when understood, will no longer feel threatening.

29

Why are cards and gifts so important to her?

Early on in my work I remember seeing a young couple who had only known each other two years and had been married just over a year. We will once again refer to them as John and Mary. When I first saw John and Mary they had just returned from celebrating their anniversary in Paris. It was Mary who had planned the trip to celebrate their first anniversary together. She had gone to a lot of trouble arranging a luxury hotel for them to enjoy the outstanding surroundings and spa facilities on offer.

Mary had chosen her anniversary card with great care and thought, she had written a loving message on it to John and as a surprise she had spent time putting together a personalized leather photo album of their first year of marriage, placing little written inscriptions alongside each photograph. Mary had made a tremendous amount of effort in the hope of them both spending five romantic and memorable days and evenings together.

The day after their arrival was their anniversary date and while John was in the bathroom Mary placed his card and the beautifully wrapped album on the bed. He spotted them straight away and was very pleased with both. She suggested they sit together and share the memories in the album she had so thoughtfully put together. They began to do this, but Mary soon became aware that John was fidgeting and becoming agitated; he also kept glancing at his watch. Mary asked him if there was something wrong and found his reply honest but rather blunt as he informed her quite sharply that they could look at the album any time and he was hungry and did not want to be late for breakfast.

Obviously Mary was hurt by this, and felt all her efforts were unappreciated. She slammed the album shut, left it on the bed and quickly got ready for breakfast. He did not pick up on her body language or how she was feeling or why, as in his logical world he was simply taking responsibility to ensure they were both fed and did not miss out on breakfast and, after all, he had only stated the truth: they could look at the album any time.

After a very silent breakfast they returned to their room. Mary was hoping at this point that John would give her a card or at least some sign to show her that her efforts were reciprocated and he had remembered to plan for the day. They finished looking at the album together at her request and John showed much pleasure in the photos and her effort. However, as nothing had been mentioned about a card for her, Mary reluctantly asked if he had got her a card. To which John replied that it was in his bag and he just needed time to write it. Mary went to the bathroom to give him time to do this.

When Mary returned from the bathroom, he handed her the card. She was immediately disappointed by the small size and quality of the envelope, which gave her prior warning that this was not a quality or special card. She sat on the bed and opened the card, which took little time to do as he had not stuck down or folded in the envelope flap. The card, as suspected, turned out to be quite unspectacular and inexpensive; she hoped he might have compensated for this by writing a loving and thoughtful message inside, but her displeasure and hurt were very obvious when she read the words 'from John'.

She felt gutted and could not think of anything she could say without causing a negative reaction. She did not want to spoil their day, but could not hold back her disappointment. The conversation that followed went like this:

Mary 'Is that it? From John! Is that the best you could do after all the effort I have made?'

John 'But it *is* from me! What did you expect me to write?'

Mary 'You could have at least written I love you or happy anniversary!'

John 'You know I love you – why do I need to write it down?'

Mary [now visibly upset] 'What planet are you on, John? You obviously do not feel like you love me or you would have written it down. The card looks like you found it in the pound shop! You could not even make the effort to buy me a decent card!'

John 'Oh, I see, this is all about money, because you wanted an expensive card! I see I am being attacked because I did not spend enough money on your card. You are always on the attack, just like your mother, never satisfied.'

The argument continued and was impossible to resolve. Both struggled to get through the day together as both believed they were the ones who had been unjustifiably attacked. Mary had taken his lack of effort as a sign he did not care, that he did not love her very much. John on the other hand was completely taken aback by her response: cards had never been of importance in his family or upbringing and he could not understand why she was making such a big thing about it. He assumed she was looking for an excuse to attack him and find fault with him, as he did not see why the message in the card could be so important to her.

It is the simple things that make women happy, and understanding why this is can prove very challenging for many men with AS. Cards, flowers and gifts for a majority of women are seen as symbolic of their partner's love because they all mean he has taken the time to think about them when he is absent from them; they show her that he considers them worth the effort it takes to choose something special for them. These tokens of his love will mean more to the woman than the fact that he might spend 12 hours a day working hard to earn them money or putting shelves up in the kitchen. She will view his work and the jobs he does as being part of life and a working relationship and will see them as something that benefits both of them and the whole family. This is very different to how she will value his effort in doing something totally personal for her, as this type of expression will say to her that she is top of his priority list and valued for the person she is. It is her emotional food and without it she will feel emotionally starved. Just a small effort made by him in this area will bring him many rewards, and one of these may be an increase in her desire to share the physical and sexual side of the relationship with him, as she will feel more emotionally satisfied and drawn to him.

For him it is again about acceptance that tokens of his love for her will be very important and crucial to feeding her emotionally in the relationship and making her happy. He must not try to figure out why, as that will cause confusion; he just needs to accept and remember that the relationship will become stronger the more effort he makes.

For some men, though, what it is they are expected to do can be very confusing and this is where the woman needs to lend a helping hand. It is important that she does not expect her partner to figure out by intuition what it is she requires from him, or by dropping hints or making sarcastic remarks, as none of these will lead to positive results. She must tell him or make him a foolproof list of what she would like, and this must be very clear, right down to the types of flowers or make of chocolates she likes. She must avoid giving only singular choices to him, for example, telling him pink roses are her favourite flower. This could result in him sticking to what he knows is guaranteed to be safe and he will probably still be buying her pink roses in years to come.

Having Asperger syndrome does not impact on intelligence and as long as men with AS are given the information they need in a clear and unambiguous manner they will soon learn to do the majority of things a woman might expect from her partner in a relationship. Whether or not he will be able to maintain the behaviour might depend strongly on whether he believes the relationship will benefit in some way from making the effort, and it *will* be an effort for him. I have seen men with AS go to great lengths to try to please their partner and ensure they remember to send them cards or make them feel special and it is important that this is not taken for granted by her and regarded as being her right. The man will be making a tremendous effort to buy, do and say things that are completely alien to him and certainly not second nature. He will be using up valuable thought space in his busy logical mind to do something that to him will feel very illogical. If he makes this effort in showing how much he loves and cares for her then it would be a foolish woman who takes his attempts for granted and does not offer any positive feedback or praise.

30

Why does she need me to keep telling her I love her?

As with the previous question this is an area which leaves most men with AS feeling bewildered and confused, and when looking at the question from a logical perspective it is not surprising. Men with AS are quite honest in their feelings, if they commit to something it is usually after much thought and most are very genuine in their commitment. Hence they will argue that, logically, what is the point in having to keep repeating, almost on a daily basis, something that they have already said and that has not, from their perspective, changed? A couple are not expected to repeat their marriage vows or early promises of commitment on a daily basis; these promises were made at the beginning of the relationship and it is a foregone conclusion that they were meant then and are meant now. So why should he keep saying 'I love you' to her and having to repeat it over and over again?

For the majority of women, however, accepting and adhering to this logical and objective way of viewing love and commitment is not an acceptable option for them. Words of love are the food they thrive on and serve to reinforce their feelings of security and self-esteem, boosting their confidence in both the relationship and their partner.

Some men with AS regard this need to be told she is loved as an indication that their partner is insecure, has emotional issues or is too needy. These assumptions are understandable as the man does not have the need for her to repeat endlessly her undying love for him. Unless he is told the contrary, he will have no reason to believe otherwise. He will take the love and commitment they share as a fact and it may not even enter his head that something might have changed or that their love for each other needs to be reinforced. Her thought process, however, is quite different as she is thinking from multiple perspectives; she will be acutely aware of not taking his love for granted and even more aware that love and commitment are vulnerable to change and the temptation can be there to stray.

She will need confirmation of his love in order to thrive in the relationship. One of the differences that exist between men and women that is often highlighted is that a man often needs a sexual connection to make him feel fulfilled and worthy in the relationship, whereas a woman needs an emotional input to make her feel she is valued and secure in his love.

For many men with AS this is a concept they may fail to understand or make sense of and this is OK, as the man does not need to understand the concept as long as he can accept it. It is the difference between the zebra and the eagle that I describe earlier in the book (see page 66). Zebras need a very different type of food and environment to thrive than an eagle and neither could survive for long if they were forced to live in each other's environment and eat each other's food.

One way for him to think about this and to help him understand her difference is to accept that she will need emotional food. As he is often the primary source of her emotional food there will only be him feeding her and its effect will soon get used up. Just as when we eat a meal, it will not be long before the body is hungry again and needs another meal. His partner will become hungry again and need more of her emotional food.

This will be different for him, as she will not be his only source and provider of food. His food is logical and he will be getting replenished from many different sources, whether that is his work or interests. He will be constantly filling up on his diet of logic and objective food.

Some men, though, will struggle with using emotional language in a way that sounds genuine and honest, and that brings us to our next question.

Rule 9

There are never enough ways to
tell her you love her.

31

How can I keep saying 'I love you' and other nice things without sounding false?

How to say 'I love you' without it sounding false is often a concern for men with AS and a question often asked. The woman may struggle with this concern if the man raises it in the counselling room and may even assume that if he fears it will sound false, then he obviously does not mean it – this is an incorrect assumption on the woman's part and often I find I need to explain to her why it can feel so difficult for him.

For the AS man to remember to tell his partner on a regular basis that he loves her will not come naturally to him. As I explained in the previous question, he will be saying he loves her on a frequent basis because he has learnt that that is what she needs him to do to reassure her. He will not be doing it because he has suddenly become overwhelmed by feelings of love and needs to express that love. It will be something that he has learned to do and it is unlikely he will have had any practice in the past of expressing these feelings in this way.

Some men with AS find it easier to write their feelings down, especially if they are also affected by alexithymia (see Question 11) which makes connecting to their feelings and then finding the words to express those feelings almost impossible. As an alternative some men use Post-it notes, text or email to express their feelings, where they have time to think the process through. Others prefer to use mediums such as colours or numbers. Colours can be useful when, for example, she asks him how he feels and he can choose from a prearranged list of colours, each of which represents a feeling he might want to express.

A colour can also be used to represent his feelings of love, while a number between 1 and 10 can be used to express how strong that feeling is at that particular moment. So, if she asks him how he is feeling he can then answer with the colour that represents love for her. If she then asks him how much he loves her, he can give his feelings a number out of 10, 10 being the strongest, and give her an accurate representation of how he feels.

For example, say the chosen colour for love was purple, and she asks how he is feeling, he could say that he is feeling lots of purple. If she then asked how purple he is feeling he could say that it is 8. For some couples just having numbers is enough to illustrate the strength of a feeling and it is something that can be used by both partners to express a whole range of feelings.

However, for some women nothing but the spoken word will suffice and his lack of response may become a bone of contention, so he may find himself being reprimanded and made to feel inadequate due to this. If this is the case and his partner knows about the effects of Asperger syndrome and alexithymia and continues to refuse to accept what this means for him, the couple perhaps should be advised to seek professional help. If this still makes no difference and a level of verbal abuse continues, then he will need to take a serious look at the relationship, and question how healthy it is and whether it is potentially detrimental to his mental and physical wellbeing.

Being affected by AS does not present with any obvious physical signs, as would be found if the person was, for example, wheelchair bound or visually impaired. AS is an invisible syndrome and, as the AS person is often of high intelligence with a capacity to get by and cope, it can be taken for granted that they have abilities they do not. Female partners will sometimes ask me how he can talk to colleagues at work or his golfing partners and yet struggles even to ask her how she feels. Often the assumption that has been formed from this is that it is a personal affront to her. This is not the case and I use the analogy of a physical disability to try to explain to the female partner what is going on. It goes something like this.

Counsellor [to the female partner] 'OK, let's imagine your partner has a severe visual impairment and he cannot see you, your body language or the expressions on your face. Would you expect him to know how you are feeling and respond accordingly? No, you would be telling him how you feel, explaining what you want from him, perhaps even physically guiding. It would be abusive to expect a person with a visual impairment to be able to work out what you needed by your silent body language and for you to punish them if they got it wrong. Likewise, having AS means your partner is mind blind and you will have to explain to him what you need. If you need him to reassure you that he loves you, you will have to ask him and allow him to answer in a language that works for him.'

Once a woman makes a connection between a physical condition which can be clearly seen and Asperger syndrome, then she will often find it easier to understand and work with the difference.

Effort will be required on both sides; allowances will need to be made for the difference in how each thinks and what each needs. He will need to find ways to convey his love for her, whether this is through the spoken word or by finding an appropriate medium; it will play a huge part in making her feel happy and more secure within his love. Some men find it easier to say 'I love you' in the dark, making it the last thing they say at night, when the couple have a cuddle before sleep, leaving her with a warm and comforting feeling that will last through the night.

She will need to accept that for him love is far more than just a spoken word and find ways to encourage him to express his feelings in a way that is comfortable for him. She will also need to avoid trying to translate his words into something negative if she feels they have not been expressed with the right amount of feeling. She cannot hold him accountable for getting his tone of voice or body language wrong, no more than she would seek to blame someone affected by dyslexia for spelling a word incorrectly or for using the wrong pronunciation. If a man with AS says 'I love you' then it is almost certain that he means it.

32

How can I tell the difference between when she just wants a hug and when she wants to have sex?

When the topic of sex comes up with the couples I work with, I sometimes find that the sexual side of the relationship is non-existent; in some cases there is no physical contact or affection shared between the couple. Exploring further I will ask what the reason for this is. Is it due to one partner not finding pleasure in tactile contact? Is it a lack of desire or stimulation? It seems contradictory when both say they enjoy physical contact, including hugs and kisses, and this is something they both miss. It is often the case that once upon a time the couple both enjoyed affection and physical contact together.

As we delve deeper the woman might state that she has withdrawn from sex because her partner cannot tell the difference between her wanting a hug and wanting to have sex. She will often be able to regurgitate a catalogue of situations when she has been upset, feeling down or poorly and has just sunk into his arms in need of his support and compassion and he has become sexually aroused and started to fondle her breasts or touch her sexually. She has found this hurtful, unsupportive and disrespectful; she will see him as being totally selfish and only seeking to satisfy his own sexual appetite while totally ignoring her emotions.

He will, meanwhile, be totally unaware that she is feeling like this as his assumption will have been that if she pushed her body against him and wanted hugging then she was trying to turn him on and wanted to make love. When he finds himself reprimanded, pushed away and rejected he will take it very personally and will, like her, feel hurt and unvalued. Without the knowledge and understanding of AS, neither will be aware of the other's interpretation of the situation, and feelings of hurt and resentment will be stored internally. If this issue is not correctly addressed and resolved then it is bound to be repeated again until both withdraw from showing any affection at all. Both will be busy trying to protect their vulnerability and avoiding the pain of feeling either used or rejected.

A woman needs hugs, kisses, strokes and touches and for her it will have absolutely nothing to do with wanting sex or needing him to arouse her for sex. The line between the two for her is very wide, strong and not to be compromised. This is a lesson about women that men with AS need to learn as quickly as possible in order to save them from causing them pain and to protect themselves from the agony of rejection and resentment.

So why is this divide between affection and sex so much stronger for women than men? The answer to this is the same whether or not the relationship is affected by Asperger syndrome: this is a difference that is about gender and upbringing and not AS. Most women are instinctively excellent nurturers and grow up being encouraged to care for and show affection towards others. Girls will be encouraged to hug each other, their parents, aunties, uncles, grandparents and so on. They will play caring games with their dolls, dress them, hug them, rock them, feed them and put them to bed. Their games will be collective and about sharing and compromising. Society encourages affectionate and nurturing behaviour in young girls.

A boy's upbringing can, however, be quite different and he will soon learn from his peers that hugging the other boys or kissing them is totally unacceptable and if affectionate behaviour continues or he displays his emotions too freely he will quickly find himself labelled as a sissy or gay.

Some young boys with AS do not always adhere to the traditional standards of masculinity (Attwood 2007) and may dress in a way that is feminine or develop mannerisms that are feminine. They will not always pick up social cues and their behaviour may be perceived as odd or feminine. They could easily become the victims of bullying and will learn very quickly to change their behaviour and distance themselves from others. As they go into late adolescence, sexual contact may be the only acceptable form of physical contact that they can be involved in, unless of course it is on the football pitch, where contact amongst men seems to be appropriate and acceptable.

If the man with AS has developed this type of script or he has grown in a household where being tactile or affectionate is non-existent or unacceptable then he will struggle with changing this script when he forms an intimate relationship, and may find it very difficult to tell the difference between a come on and her just wanting a hug. Often the difference is revealed in the context of the situation, for example, if she has just had some bad news or if the hug is because she is upset or feeling poorly then it is unlikely it will mean sex is on the agenda.

This is where having AS does start to play a part, because a non-AS man would find it easier to read the peripheral signals surrounding the hug and be able to tell the difference. He would know that sexual contact between them is not going to make her feel better if she is upset or feeling down. It might make him feel better in that situation but he would be able to separate his needs from hers.

For the man with AS this will not always happen and he could soon find his advances being rejected. One way round this is for him to have a rule that unless she touches him sexually or asks him to make love to her he will never presume sex is on the agenda. Even if the couple are in bed together and things are becoming passionate I would still suggest he asks her if she wants to make love.

As long as she understands why he is asking her and does not misinterpret this to mean that he is only making love with her because she wants him to, and can see this as his way of being respectful, then it will take all the guesswork out of sex and save both much pain. Men, unlike women, would find it very hard to fake sexual desire or arousal and if he did not desire her or want to have sex with her, then the physical signs would be more than obvious as he would be unlikely to achieve or maintain an erection. (This is presuming there was not a physical or medical cause for erectile dysfunction such as taking certain medications or being overtired or stressed; this, however, would need to be checked out with a general practitioner.)

Showing respect in a relationship will gain respect back and if the AS man never presumes his partner wants sex, but is always willing to offer non-sexual hugs and kisses, then she will feel respected and respect his feelings in return. He may find that by him taking this approach she will feel encouraged to be closer to him and may become keener to engage in sexual relations with him. Once again understanding and accepting will result in benefits for both.

33

Why won't she have sex with me?

In my research (Aston 2001) I found that 50 per cent of the couples that filled in my questionnaires had no sexual contact at all. Often by the time a couple get to see me, this has been the way for some years and both have come to accept the relationship as purely platonic. Sometimes the AS man has withdrawn from all physical contact because he is finding that the sharing of sex with his partner has become stressful and emotionally overwhelming, so much so that he cannot cope with that side of the relationship. His fear of getting it wrong will actually cause it to go wrong and he may soon withdraw from sharing sex altogether and resort to self-masturbation as an easier and less complex alternative.

It may be that his partner will have raised the topic many times and in most cases she will not have received any explanation from him for why he does not want her sexually. He will not have answered her questions because he is unable to find the words to express how he feels, or because he is fearful of discussing his feelings in case they provoke a row. However, she may not know this and so will be left feeling very hurt and rejected by his refusal both to discuss the matter and to make love with her.

She is unlikely to hide these feelings of hurt and rejection from him and they will probably be expressed with anger and or resentment. She will be desperately looking for an answer to explain why he is rejecting and avoiding her sexually, and she is likely to assume that if he is not having sex with her, then he must be getting it from somewhere else, which could lead to the conclusion that her partner must be having an affair or is gay. She will be desperately looking for a reason so she can make sense of what is happening. She will rapidly find herself struggling with both the emotional and physical deprivation, her self-esteem will diminish, and both partners will find themselves in a very lonely and unhappy place.

When this happens it will be very difficult for the couple to resolve the issues without professional help and, if possible, they should explore the possibility of seeking counselling or psychosexual therapy with a therapist who has an understanding of the effects of Asperger syndrome in a relationship.

However, it is not always the man who withdraws from the sexual side of the relationship; indeed, in the majority of cases it is the woman who has withdrawn from sex. When it is this way round it is unlikely to have been addressed or discussed between them. Unlike her reaction to the situation described above, which was one of challenging and questioning, he will not have challenged her or endeavour to discover why she has withdrawn from sex with him. The reason for this lack of challenge on his part is often his fear of confrontation; rather than risk asking her what is wrong, he will just suffer in silence while his inner resentment builds up.

The woman's withdrawal from sex with her partner can be for various reasons. It may be that she is finding sex painful or uncomfortable, or she may be tired or feeling unwell. Normally these issues will be short lived and likely to be resolved quickly. If, however, her refusal is long term, then it is most likely that she feels he is not emotionally feeding her: he does not make the effort to give her enough time or attention that goes towards making her feel special and of value in the lead up to sex.

Women describe how their partner may attempt to initiate sex from the 'cold position'. This implies that there were no nice words or deeds, no wooing or romancing of her; rather, he went straight into sex mode and may have begun by fondling her sexually or pushing himself against her with an obvious erection. She is unlikely to find these advances flattering or stimulating if her emotions are feeling neglected. His attentions will result in her feeling she is being used as a sexual object to satisfy his own needs and as a consequence she will be likely to reject him. If the issue is not addressed, then both will back off and before long sex will be off the agenda altogether.

When a couple come to see me, it soon becomes apparent that the issues over sex have never been discussed or brought up between them. It is often only in the safety of the counselling room that the topic will be raised and discussed by them for the first time. It will often be revealed that he did not raise the topic for fear of it leading to a confrontation between them and it is likely that she will have interpreted this as him not caring.

His silence may have reinforced her belief that he just wanted her for sex, and unless sex was on the agenda he could not be bothered to talk to her. Until now it seems the couple dealt with the issues in silence and neither sought to resolve them or to question why things weren't right. This silent pact between them could have been ongoing for years and neither will have any idea of how it is impacting on the other.

In other cases I discover that she has tried to raise the issue and told him that she needs to be made to feel special or to feel emotionally supported before she would be willing to make love with him. He will have heard this message and probably felt quite confused as to what this meant or what he should do; unless such a message is delivered with a full set of instructions, it is likely he will do nothing. It is often only within the safety of the therapy room that she will, for the first time, get to hear from him about how the lack of sexual contact has made him feel, and this may come as quite a surprise to her.

I often find within my work that just as men with AS struggle to understand the emotional side of their female partners, it is frequently the case that the female partner does not understand the sexual side of the AS man. When an AS man is committed and with a woman he is physically and intellectually attracted to, he will be sexually loyal and rarely seek to have sex elsewhere. Sex with his partner will not be a means to an end and it will not just be sex for the sake of sex. To him sex will be the one way he will feel able to demonstrate to her how much he loves her. This is how he gains his intimacy; making love with her will, for him, be worth more than a hundred handwritten love notes and twice as many words expressing his love. Making love is about doing, not saying: the AS man is happy and far more confident with doing than finding words to express how he feels. Sadly, this is often misunderstood by her, which is not surprising as she will be looking for affirmation of his love in a very different way.

It is said that women need to feel emotionally close to desire sex; unfortunately, making his partner feel emotionally close is not something that the AS man is able to do with ease. This can lead to her rejecting him and in turn leave him without any way of showing his love for her; it also leaves him feeling stripped bare of his confidence and self-worth. He will feel her rejection very deeply but will be unlikely to voice this and will simply accept that he is unwanted and undesired. He will very quickly withdraw and distance himself even more.

The problem is that she will read his distance as affirmation that he does not want to make the effort to make her feel emotionally supported. She will view his withdrawal as confirmation that all he wanted from her was sex and, now there is no sex, he is not interested in her at all. She will have been hoping that her withdrawal would have conveyed the message to him that he needs to make more effort to show her emotionally that he loves her. She will have in effect been playing a mind game, without realising it was with a partner who cannot read minds.

He will not look beyond her actions and these will spell out to him that she did not want his love; he will not be able to imagine the alternatives or figure out what she wants him to do. He is unable to put himself in her place, in her shoes; he is only able to put himself in his shoes. Anything else will be guesswork and, without definite spoken instructions from her on what she wants him to do, he won't be able to work it out.

Lack of emotional support, however, is not the only reason a woman may withdraw from sex. In some cases it has come down to personal hygiene. When this subject has been raised in the therapy room, it has been expressed that she feels her partner does not shower enough or clean his teeth on a regular basis. In this case it is important that the man takes responsibility to keep himself clean, especially if he wishes to share a bed and his body with a partner. If he is not prepared to make an effort in this department, then his partner is justified in saying no to physical contact.

If a man finds himself in the situation that his partner has withdrawn from sex, he will need to approach the subject with his partner. If he feels that to try to verbalise this would be too stressful or too risky, then he could either write it in a letter or email or suggest they both go to counselling together. The longer he avoids the topic the harder it will be to deal with. He will need to be aware of and respect that her emotional needs are very important and that she will feel undervalued if they are not met. If he can make the effort to listen to what she has to say, to take her needs seriously and do what he can to fulfil them, then his rewards will be all the greater.

If she feels he is not emotionally feeding her or spending enough time making her feel special, then he will need to ask her to tell him what he might do to make her feel special. It will be important that her expectations of him are realistic and that she is not expecting him to go to extremes of romantic passion. If her expectations are too high she may well be disappointed. This is why it is so important that the couple talk together and explore avenues that they might try together. It is up to both to make the other feel special, and not just the role of one or other. He has needs too; it would be an error to presume that all he needs is her body. He needs to feel desired, wanted and loved too. For many men with AS, it is not only how they achieve at work that fulfils their self-esteem in the family; it is also how well they can satisfy their partner sexually.

However, if he finds that no matter what he does or tries, she still refuses to have any physical contact with him and there is no medical reason why she cannot, then he will have to decide what he wants. If the relationship gives him enough to benefit him, despite it being platonic, then he may well be able to continue.

And then there were three...

Starting a family brings many inevitable changes and challenges to the lives of any couple. In the case of the AS/non-AS relationship, the birth of their first child is often the time that many couples identify as when things started to go wrong and fall apart in their relationship.

Having a child is a major transition time for any couple, as they find themselves moving from their role as a couple to that of being parents; instead of being David and Susan they now become Emily's mum and dad!

Another little person or persons moves into their lives, a little person who initially is totally dependent on them, very demanding, makes a lot of noise, needs a lot of care and attention day and night and, for a while, gives very little back. This will tax any couple and push them to their limits at a time when they are affected by multiple transitions, sleep deprivation, and very little time for themselves let alone each other!

Couples choose to have a child for various reasons. In some cases it is to fix a weak or troubled relationship, an idea that is completely flawed – the reality is that if the relationship is troubled before the baby was born, it will be even more troubled and under pressure after the birth of a baby. I would advise any couple to consider carefully together why they want a child and to explore together realistically what this will mean to them and their relationship.

Children take up a lot of time and they are a very expensive addition to any household, which could put a family that is already struggling financially under a lot of strain. Sometimes children arrive sooner than planned – the couple may not be ready to become parents and will not feel they have had enough time to grow together. It is worthwhile considering this before taking risks with birth control or rushing in too quickly.

On the other hand, children are described as a blessing by many parents and the joy children can bring is tenfold compared to the effort it takes to look after them and care for them. It will not always feel like this, though, especially in the beginning (and it can take several months or longer of sleepless nights and 24/7 childcare to reach the point that the couple feel they are getting something back from their child).

OK, so I think I have spelt out realistically the downside of having children and that it is important to have a child for the right reasons and with no illusions taken from the baby adverts! This is advice to any couple who are considering having a child and applies equally to all couples, whether or not one parent is affected by Asperger syndrome. I am not of the opinion that having Asperger syndrome should have any detrimental effect on a person's capacity to rear children and be a loving and caring parent. Once again this is about who the person is, their personality and the reasons they are having children. What is important for couples affected by AS is that they are totally aware of what that means in terms of their ability to empathise with and mindread their children. If the understanding is there and the couple work as a team then their children will receive a good upbringing.

However, I do find that there are some issues that seem to repeat themselves amongst couples and I am frequently asked the same questions by fathers with AS, so I have tried to address some of those in this book. In this part I have referred to the parents as the mother and father, though it is sometimes the case that one of the parents is a step parent, or both may be adoptive parents or foster parents. The questions and answers will apply equally to all these possible scenarios. It would be impossible to cover all eventualities in this book and the questions chosen are the most common that come up. They will not give answers to all the issues that might arise and will not apply to everyone, as all people and their children are unique.

34

We have recently had our first child. I feel my whole life has been turned upside down. My wife has become totally unpredictable; one minute she is happy and the next she is crying her eyes out. What's wrong with her?

The birth of a child is a major time of transition and a couple will be learning to fit into their new roles as Mum and Dad. This is a time when each will need the support of their partner. If it is she who is the primary carer, as it often is, for financial and practical reasons, then this is a time she will need her partner more than ever. His support, love and care will be fundamental in how she gets through this initial stage of childcare. More than ever she will need him to be there, not just for practical reasons but also for his emotional support, which will be critical for her now. Her hormones will be causing her to experience great waves of ups and downs. One minute her partner will find her up and coping and another minute she will be in a flood of tears telling him she is a total failure as a woman and a mother. She will need his emotional support more than ever to help her survive the avalanche of mixed up hormones and emotions she will be experiencing.

Following the birth, especially in the case of a difficult birth, caesarean section or if she required stitches, the mother is likely to be in pain, exhausted and possibly limited physically in what she is able to do. This coupled with the whole hormonal upheaval may leave her feeling emotional, teary and possibly anxious or depressed. The father at the same time may feel overwhelmed by the responsibility of a new baby and the many changes it can cause. He will feel he is suddenly no longer the centre of her attention and that everything is about the baby. He may feel unable to get physically close to his partner and may start to feel quite neglected in the relationship.

In answer to the question, there is nothing wrong with the female partner, and many females can feel and behave as described in the early weeks following the birth. If, however, her mood swings worsen or she continues to express symptoms such as being down, tearful and unmotivated, reporting finding it difficult to cope with the new baby, not sleeping, having little appetite, complaining of stomach pains, headaches, panic attacks or blurred vision and generally neglecting herself, and this continues for longer than two weeks, then she must seek medical advice as she could be suffering from postnatal depression.

One problem that can be encountered in the AS/non-AS relationship during the early weeks following the birth is that the emotional support and comfort she is seeking may not be within the remit of the AS man to give. This in turn will exaggerate her feelings of coping alone, especially if she is unaware that her partner is likewise struggling and feeling out of his depth trying to deal with the emotional demands he suddenly finds made upon him.

If ever I find there is a specific time that an AS man decides to become a workaholic and spends all his time at work, or a time when he throws himself into a hobby such as running or going down the gym, this will be the time. This may be due to him trying to find a role or wanting to do something to support her and his new family. He may work harder to increase their financial security or he may decide they need a new bathroom or the outside area of the house needs to be safer. Unfortunately, while it might help him to feel more purposeful and less stressed, it will result in her feeling abandoned and neglected in her time of greatest need.

Her feelings will be of disillusionment, as his emotional and physical distance would not have been what she wanted or imagined would happen. She may have imagined that it would be a time of bonding between her and her partner, of them sharing this little new life together. Instead she could find herself taking most of the responsibility for the child alone and to make it worse she will find he will argue that his reasons are quite justified. He may not be able to understand why she is so miserable when she finally has what she wanted so much: a baby.

It is important for the AS man to take on board that it is not just her baby, it is their baby – without him the baby would not be there. His partner really needs him now and he will need to dedicate some of his time to her and their new baby. He may say he does not know what she wants him to do and if this is the case then he will need to ask what it is she wants. For example, does she want him to take baby out for a walk in the local park, is there anything she needs from the shops, would she like him to bath the baby, make them both dinner or simply give her lots of extra hugs? Just by taking a little bit of time and showing he cares, in a way that meets her needs, can make a huge difference to how she will be feeling.

Having Asperger syndrome does not determine how good a parent a person will be: that is about who they are and their personality. Some AS men struggle at this time and find babies bewildering, fragile and needy; other men will take to the father role like a duck to water and will find no problem in fulfilling it. What is important is to remember that a couple are in this together, and both have a role to play in bringing up their child.

The roles are equal and both need to share the hard times as well as the easy and fun times. The baby stage is not easy and can put a lot of demands on a couple. They will need to work as a team and the man must remember that he will be feeling far more physically and emotionally able than she after the birth. Having a baby plays havoc with her hormones and it will take two years before her body physically returns to normal.

35

Our baby seems to scream all the time and I cannot cope with the noise. I am not getting any sleep. My partner does not understand how hard it is for me and gets angry if I complain. Why?

Sensory sensitivity can be a major issue for some people affected by Asperger syndrome and I have found that a heightened sensitivity to noise, rather than the other four senses, is the most problematic and common concern that is raised by the men I see.

Despite sensitivity to noise being the most common complaint I receive, how it impacts on the individual can vary greatly. For some men it may be high-pitched noises, such as fire engines, drills, the Underground or even a dog's bark that will be described as excruciating and intolerable. For other men it can be background noise which they find distracting, such as a ticking clock or people talking in the background. Distracting noises such as these can make holding a conversation and maintaining concentration almost impossible. The most difficult places are reported to be noisy atmospheres that are flooded with background sounds, say a restaurant or a pub.

In other cases someone with AS may find that they have problems even processing information or retaining attention in an environment that is noisy, as they will have difficulty tuning out from the noise and find they are easily distracted by it.

When noise feels overwhelming some men will have to leave the room and find somewhere quiet to avoid spiralling downwards into a meltdown. Consequently they may find themselves accused by their partners of being unsociable or unreasonable, but this is not the case. I have had men describe being able to hear sounds that other people cannot pick up on, such as dog whistles and cat deterrents; these noises are not even audible to the average ear, so when a man with AS is faced with a baby that will not stop crying, it can have quite a detrimental effect on him and his capacity to cope and function.

If this is an issue within a relationship it can be very difficult to solve without the female partner being very understanding and sympathetic as to the reasons why. If she does not understand about Asperger syndrome and its effects, she is likely to believe he is making an excuse to walk away when their baby cries. She will feel abandoned by him and feel that his behaviour is unreasonable and selfish, especially if he should become irritable with her about it. Her reactions are understandable as she is likely to be doing all she can to pacify the baby and settle him or her down.

It is plausible that she will feel upset and unsupported by him if she is not aware of why he is walking away and abandoning her. Although their baby's crying will still have an impact on her, it will be different to how it affects him. Their baby's crying will trigger in her an instinctual reaction that will motivate her to respond to the crying and seek to find ways to soothe the baby and meet his or her needs.

If a couple have a baby who seems to cry almost constantly it can make life very difficult for both of them. They will both be feeling the effects of sleep deprivation, though if she is breastfeeding their child it is likely she will be getting less sleep than her partner. It is no wonder she reacts when he complains how tired he is when she is the one who has been up all night.

Unfortunately, there is no short cut around this one and it is a stage in babyhood that will have to be worked through together. It will of course help if she has an understanding of sensory sensitivity and the reality of the effect it can have on her partner. Without this she is unlikely to be able to offer any support or understanding of the situation to him.

Some couples choose to sleep in separate rooms during this time if the space is available; this way she is able to feed the

What Men with AS Want to Know About Women, Dating and Relationships

baby without disturbing her partner's sleep. Some men have fitted themselves with ear plugs to try to cut out the sounds or play music through an iPod. Both will need to experiment and find what works for them.

What needs to be remembered is that if the woman is prepared to understand how the noise of the baby's crying is affecting him, then he must find other ways to compensate her for the fact that she will be the one pacifying the infant when it is crying. This is especially so if the infant cries for long periods in the night. Maybe he could take on more of the household chores, offer to make dinner or go out and get a take away for them both to give her time to relax or do other things.

The couple could arrange a baby sitter so they can go out and have some quality time together. This of course depends on the availability of help, and the baby's age and feeding schedule, and these options may not always be possible in the early days. This can be a hard time for both partners and each will need the support and consideration of the other. Tempers may be short and emotions may be volatile. It is, though, only for a time; the crying will stop.

36

I spend all day at work and when I get home my partner expects me to take on the childcare, yet she has been at home all day. This feels unreasonable. Is it?

It must feel really hard to have spent all day at work and to come home to a tired and distraught partner, demanding and noisy children and a multitude of household chores that need doing. Some men with AS describe a situation where they come home and are instantly given a list of jobs to do, and this might not change as the children grow – all that will change will be the tasks on the list. They may find that in time jobs like bathing the baby will be replaced with taking their daughter to and from her ballet class.

Sharing the household tasks can be a contentious issue, especially if he feels very strongly that looking after the children and housework is down to the female. The reason for this belief is often his upbringing, especially if he was reared in a household where his mother took total charge of the children and the house while his father went out to work and earned the money.

In the case where the men are sole earners some describe that they feel they lose out all round and complain that as well as working hard to earn money, so their wife can be at home to look after the children, they are also coming home to a house of chaos, clutter and more jobs. Some men believe their partner should be the one doing these household jobs as she is the one who has been at home all day.

I can understand how this conclusion is reached logically as it must feel quite illogical that she has not been able to complete all the household jobs throughout the day. However, what he may not be taking into account is that she is not alone throughout the day; she is in the company of, possibly, a baby, a toddler or a young child, or in some cases all three. Looking after young children, keeping them safe and cleaning up after them is a full-time job and in many cases leaves little room for anything else. I see women who are verging on the edge of severe self-neglect. They are tired, worn out, uninspired and in desperate need of some 'me time' and a bit of pampering. This still applies even if the woman has chosen to return to work part or full time following maternity leave; she will still be feeling tired and very alone.

Many women describe how they are envious of the fact that their partner is able to just walk out of the house, and drive away. He spends the day with adults, doing adult stuff, having adult conversations and having coffee and lunch breaks. She may feel quite isolated and neglected by her partner; he may not always remember to call her through the day and ask how she is getting on.

He is unlikely to come home and ask about her day as he may consider it intellectually boring. There may be days when she feels down or unwell and yet still finds herself coping alone because his job is too important to take time off. Until a parent is in the situation of being the sole child and house carer throughout the day it is hard to imagine the effect. Even when her partner listens as she tries to justify how tired and wretched she feels he will still not understand. In his desire to fix it he might suggest she tries to find time to relax and sit down through the day – this will show her he does not understand.

It is likely that by the time he comes home she feels she has had all she can stand and may feel resentful that she was the one who, often for financial reasons, gave up her career to look after the children. She may resent the fact that all the childcare has become her responsibility when, after all, the children belong to both of them. So, yes, he is likely to be greeted by a very tired and disgruntled partner who will be more than eager to pass on the childcare and chores to him. She will not feel any guilt over this because, after all, her day does not end at five: it is ongoing, sometimes round the clock, so why should he be privileged to walk in through the door and enjoy the luxury of having nothing to do?

This is how it feels from her perspective, which, when you look at it separately from his, makes as much sense and logic as his does. Both are tired at the end of the day, and some men find work uses up all their resources and they really feel wrecked by the time they get home. Many men just want to be alone and have time to digest and process all that has occurred in the day. However, he is not living alone and has made the decision to be in a relationship and have children, so other options need to be explored so that both can find some time for themselves and each other.

What can be achieved to improve the situation depends on the couple's circumstances and the ages of the children. I have found that sometimes the best answer is to develop an all or nothing approach, because then there is no blurring of the boundaries and each will know what they are doing and on what nights they are doing it. How this works is that each will take it in turns to do the childcare in the evening after he arrives home. What childcare entails will have to be determined by each in the relationship; it could mean cooking the children's tea, feeding them, bathing them, reading a story and putting them to bed. Whatever the arrangement, each will take responsibility for the children's care on alternate nights. So if, for instance, Monday is his night, then it will be for her to do what she wishes in this time. She might choose to pop out to the hairdressers or to go for a walk, or she may simply choose to lie down and catch up on some sleep. Tuesday would then be her turn and in this time her partner is free to do as he chooses, whether that is to go to the gym, spend time on the internet or just chill out and read. This way both will have a few hours alone and the time will be equally shared.

Some couples extend this arrangement to the weekends with each choosing on either a Saturday or a Sunday to be the one to get up with the children and take care of them in order to allow the other partner to have a lie in. Sharing in this way can work much better than both sharing the jobs when he comes home, which results in neither getting a complete break for themselves.

Of course there are some circumstances where this will not be practical or possible. For example, in the case of a breastfeeding infant the father can only take on some of the duties. Also, if the couple have more than one child, especially when both are still very young, it may be difficult for one partner to do all the bedtime routine.

This system is, however, flexible and a couple may use it for only one night each in the week or for half of the bedtime routine. For example, one partner could do dinner while the other does bathtime. Each couple will need to sit down and work out fairly together what works for them and their particular lifestyle and situation. What is important is that it takes both partners' needs into account and both are able to get some valuable time for themselves.

37

My partner said she cannot trust me to look after the children. I would never hurt the children so why is she saying this?

Leaving the children in their partner's sole care is an issue often raised by the women I see and for the majority it is a very genuine concern, and certainly not without good cause. For some men it feels she is being vindictive or accusatory; this, though, is rarely the reality, as her concern is sincere and is not being used as an excuse to turn the children against him or limit his time alone with them. This could not be further from the truth, as she is probably quite eager for someone to take them off her hands for a while and give her a break.

Having children will bring out the most protective instincts in a mother and if one takes lessons from the animal kingdom it is a fact that it is far more likely to be the female of the species that defends their young and if necessary dies in the attempt. It is a common rule when in the countryside that you should never place yourself between a mare or cow and their young as this could result in dire consequences. There are accounts of farmers and walkers being attacked by animals for unwittingly breaking this rule and leading the mother animal to believe they were posing a threat to her foal or calf.

The majority of women are not dissimilar and will protect their children from anything and anybody who they perceive to be a threat, and that includes the children's father. This is not because the women I see believe he is a threat to the children, far from it, and the women I speak to would be all too ready to confirm that. They are more than aware that Dad loves their children as much as they do and would never intentionally cause them harm or put them at risk. However, being a parent with

Asperger syndrome can make it harder to figure out some of the more subtle rules of parenting.

The issue of trusting the man with the childcare is sometimes raised by his partner and not always when the children are young. It can also be, for example, when they are older and he takes them camping or on some other pursuit. The two main concerns that are most often raised by the children's mother are, first, the problem that her partner could get distracted and not be aware of the dangers that could pose a risk to the children and, second, having expectations of the children which are higher than their physical or mental capacities.

Looking first at the issue of distraction, as this is the most common concern raised by the children's mother, this is caused by her partner getting distracted and not seeing the dangers that just turning your back for two minutes can put young children in. Young children need to be supervised and watched constantly. The environment the children are in has to be made as child safe as possible and the carer of the children must be able to predict what might pose a danger or threat to them, especially as often the danger is not immediately apparent.

I have been given examples by women that vary greatly, however, the underlying effect is the same. For example, one woman described her partner getting so focused on a DIY project he was working on that he failed to notice his four-year-old son occupying himself by taking out and playing with the contents of Dad's tool box. Although this certainly kept the young boy entertained while Dad did a grand job of fixing the doors to the new kitchen units his son could have seriously hurt himself playing with potentially dangerous tools. His partner was understandably far from happy when she returned from the shops, and walked into the kitchen as their young son swung a hammer in the air.

The second issue is the AS partner's difficulty in relating to the developmental level the child is at. For example, a father took his seven-year-old son out on his bicycle and as he was a keen off-road cyclist he took his son to one of his favourite tracks. It had been raining and the terrain was quite muddy and waterlogged.

This was not a problem for the boy's father and he was soon engrossed in his favourite pastime. What he failed to take into account was that his young son's ability to handle his bike in such adverse terrain was limited and before very long his son misjudged a bend and went flying through the air into a tree.

The outcome was that his son had a very nasty fall and broke his arm; his mother was very distressed about this and was angry that his father took him into a situation he could not physically manage. Her trust in his capacity to look after the children was lost and took a while to return. The lack of being able to relate to the child's developmental stage can equally apply to the intellectual and cognitive level of development, such as the ability to solve mathematical equations or to apply philosophical reasoning.

Being a parent with Asperger syndrome will place an importance on knowing what the weak spots are and to be able to take advice from the non-AS parent. He will need to learn to listen to what she says and even though this may feel undermining or difficult it is far better than the consequence of being responsible for something going wrong. It does, though, need to be mentioned that even with vigilant supervision and when the environment has been made safe there will still be incidents when children have accidents and in these cases no parent is to blame.

Even if AS is taken out of the equation it will still often be found that in the couple it is the mother who is more aware of their children's competences and more in tune to any possible dangers that may pose a threat to them. In most couple relationships both will work together, being aware that they each come with an equally relevant set of benefits to prosper the relationship and the children. He will often be working hard to provide the essentials and comforts his family need to develop and this is worthy of praise and acknowledgment. Likewise she will be bringing her instincts, intuition and empathy, which will help create a more trusting and safer environment for everyone. Working together and accepting that both aspects play an important role in the upbringing of the children and neither is of lesser relevance than the other will result in a healthier and more harmonious atmosphere for their children to develop in.

Rule 10

Never get distracted while the kids
are in your care.

38

I feel totally on the outside and alienated from the family. It feels like it is them and me, yet my partner gets angry and accuses me of not being involved enough with them. Who is right?

Both partners are probably right in how they feel: she feels alone and unsupported and he feels excluded and alienated from the family; neither is to blame for what is causing the other to feel discontented. It is again down to both seeing things very differently and not understanding what that difference is.

Let us start with his perception of how he is alienated and on the outside of the family; this is a perception that is commonly expressed to me by people with AS. When I enquire further I often discover that he quite enjoys his own company and considers himself to have always been a loner. Following this I will ask my clients to consider the following carefully: do they, despite trying to be part of a group or social circle, find themselves being excluded and put on the outside by others or is it a case that they decide to put themselves on the outside and not participate in the group or social circle? The answer to both of these questions is actually yes.

Not for all, but for some with AS, there may be the feeling that if only they had close friends then everything would be all right. I continue our discussion by asking the man to tell me what he has tried to do to make friends and build up his social circle, and what I discover is often 'nothing'. I ask, 'Well, how are you going to make friends if you do not go out and put yourself in a social situation?' I may be told in reply that he does not want to go out and spend time with others or that there is nowhere he wants to go. Other reasons I am given is that he is too busy to socialise and all his spare time might be spent on his interest, which could be going to the gym, running, browsing the internet or playing video games, all of which tend to be solitary pursuits. I may suggest that he joins a social group or find a hobby that involves other people and often I find that this never comes to anything.

So what is going on? Does the AS person really want to make friends, when their words say they do and their actions say the opposite? Why is there such a discrepancy between the idea and the reality? For some the fear of suffering rejection as they have done in the past is so great that they avoid social interaction altogether. For others it is that the stress and hard work entailed in trying to make friendships is so great that the reward of having a large social circle is not worth the cost. For yet others the real desire to have friends may not be a priority for them yet the pressures and ideals society places on friendships will result in them feeling they have to make friends in order to be happy.

I see so many young people and adolescents with AS who try so hard to fit in and develop a broad social circle because that is what they are told they have to do to be popular and acceptable. However, the cost to them and the amount of energy it requires for them to do this is tremendous.

In order to try to form friendships the person with AS would have to step out of their comfort zone, they would have to take unpredictable risks and go through the traumas of trying to do small talk, mindread and appear socially adept. It is very hard for people who have a fully developed theory of mind and natural social skills to imagine just how hard it is for someone who does not have these abilities to meet up with and socialise with other people. Trying to imagine the amount of stress and anxiety it can cause someone with AS is very hard to do.

One way for a non-AS person to envisage this is to imagine finding themselves in another culture and amongst a group of people whose rules and ways are totally different to theirs. Their eyes are hidden with dark glasses and it is impossible to know whether they are friendly or hostile, as they do not give any indication as to what their intentions are. If the non-AS person tries to approach them and communicate they will not be able to tell whether they have got it right or not, or whether they are liked or not by this strange group of people. In a situation like this the non-AS person would soon find themselves feeling very anxious, highly stressed and monitoring every word they said for fear of saying the wrong thing and upsetting or offending someone.

This is rather what it is like for someone with AS; being in a social situation can feel stressful, uncomfortable and hard work. Some with AS can find themselves feeling totally exhausted at the end of a social event and it is not uncommon for a woman to disclose how she found her AS partner asleep or missing, having left the social gathering.

For some people with AS making friends is just not on their agenda and they make the decision to enjoy their time alone and not attempt to have a relationship. They are content with this decision. The majority, though, do want a relationship and do manage to make the effort and find themselves a partner. To do this will take much effort on their part and it can sometimes be the fact that this effort is quite short lived and not maintained and this is what has happened in one case I have in mind. In the beginning he felt able to make the effort to be part of the relationship and family, but after a while, when the relationship became more demanding, with the birth of children, he felt his resources ran out and he distanced himself in order to keep his stress levels down. He was not aware that distancing himself would result in his feelings of being alienated from her and his family.

So, looking now at the female perspective in this situation, she will be aware that he is limiting his time spent with her and the family, and will have initially encouraged him to be part of the family unit. However, she will find that whatever effort she makes it will not have made any difference: he will still be standing on the outside looking in, and over time she will give up trying to bring him into the family unit. She will change her mindset and take on the view that if he wants to be part of the family he will be, and that there is no point trying to include him in the family when it makes no difference. If she does not understand AS then she will become angry because she will believe his distance is intentional and his choice; she will not understand that he finds it hard work to figure out what is expected of him and what he should do to join in, especially when he does not have any idea how to play with the children or quite how he should talk to them.

If the children become aware that it is always Mum who spends time with them or is the one who plays with them they will soon start to look to her to be with them more than Dad, and this could reinforce his feelings of being on the outside. If the issue is not addressed then over time feelings of resentment will build up on both sides and the end result is that she will feel she is a single parent bringing up the children alone.

A couple who find themselves in this situation clearly need to talk and decide exactly what roles each wishes to take in childcare. This will, of course, be based on the time each has to offer, which will not always be equal. Ways that he can feel more connected and part of the family need to be explored, and the decisions that are made need to be practical and doable – there is no point in overestimating and consequently being disappointed. For instance, the AS man may like to take his children to the cinema every week, or take them swimming and teach them to be excellent swimmers. He will need to explore what is possible for them to do together, and if his time with the children can also involve an activity he is interested in then all the better. If there is more than one child he might also explore the possibility of spending time with them separately, which will make it easier for him to focus and manage; it is also good for the children as it takes away the need to compete for Dad's attention. What is most important is that the time spent together is quality time as that is far more important to children than quantity.

39

Why does she say I am too serious with the children/grandchildren?

Playing naturally with children requires being able to access and utilise a very vivid imagination and knowing how to apply this appropriately to the child's developmental stage. As well as being creative, playing with children also requires 'acting silly' and not worrying about what anyone thinks about this.

Being able to do both these things could present a problem to the man with AS. In addition to this, some of the men I see can be quite pedantic and will, without realising it, find themselves correcting their young child's baby talk and lack of appropriate grammar or tense. They are unlikely to use baby talk back to their children or use pet names or, for some, even abbreviated versions of names. For example, if a child's name is Elisabeth she will be called Elisabeth even if the rest of the family use terms such as Liz or Lizzie.

Women have described situations with the children where he has struggled with relaxing and just enjoying the moment as it happens; he has taken things far too seriously, missing the humour in the situation. For example, a woman described how they were celebrating a family Christmas at home. She had cooked and served up a fantastic dinner with all the trimmings. Her parents were present and so was her husband's mother. In addition there were their two children, aged 11 and 9.

They had finished dinner and retired to the lounge, where they were enjoying coffee and liqueurs while watching the children open presents – so far so good. One of the presents had been a game which involved using an egg timer. The game was played in teams of two and the opposing side took charge of the egg timer and was responsible for saying when the time to answer the question was up. The questions were mixed and aimed at various age groups. Mum and Dad were a team of two and it was their turn to play against their nine-year-old son who had teamed up with Grandma. The question was asked and the egg timer set. The boy gave the answer just as the egg timer ran out. The other adults were willing to let this drop as the boy was so pleased to have got the answer but Dad immediately told him that the time was up and he could not have the point. He would not let this drop, despite the boy getting upset and the other adults getting annoyed. This spoiled the game and ruined the mood of the evening. He refused to apologise, stating that he was in the right as the egg timer had run out.

It was as though the boy's father had completely forgotten that the game was for fun and his young son at the age of nine was not going to be overly concerned with the trivialities of a few grains of sand. His son was not intentionally cheating, he was excited and enjoying the game. His father did apologise the next day for his overreaction but not for his reasons.

When bringing up children it is important to be aware of what they can and cannot do and to have realistic expectations of how much they are able to achieve cognitively and physically. This does seem to be an issue that is often raised and I have been given examples of children being expected to understand difficult mathematical equations, to be able to compete with Dad in sports that the young person was not physically able to perform, to understand complex strategic moves in games such as chess and to apply the correct etiquette at the dining table, and being constantly corrected for mispronunciation of words or using the wrong word.

It will normally be Mum who will come to the child's rescue and put herself in the firing line by confronting the AS man over his unrealistic expectations. She does not do this to put him down or show him up in front of the children; it is because she is better able to understand the developmental stage their child is at. She is aware of what they can and cannot do and she will be very aware if their father has expectations that are beyond what the child is capable of.

In an AS/non-AS relationship both will be bringing different qualities to the relationship and it is important to value the qualities each have to offer. These qualities will also count towards being a parent. Although having AS will not mean the parent loves or cares for their child any more or less, it may mean they will struggle with instinctively knowing and understanding what their children's needs are and how best to meet them; this will especially apply if the child is not affected by Asperger syndrome.

Liane Holliday Willey discusses her role as a mother in her interview with Professor Attwood (Holliday Willey and Attwood 2000) and describes how, when she recognised her difficulty in understanding her non-Asperger daughter, she went to great lengths to read books on child development so she could understand her child better and give her the best possible upbringing she could. The AS parent may see their children as mini adults and overestimate their abilities. It is therefore important to check things out with the non-AS partner, who will be a better judge of what the children need and what their capabilities are.

The AS man needs to value the advice his partner gives and listen to what she is saying without feeling she is undermining him. She is trying to do what is best for the children and also to make the relationship he has with his children stronger and more appropriate for them all. Most mothers will encourage a good rapport between their children and their father; this is important for him and especially for the emotional development and security of the children.

Just as she has the quality of being in tune with the children and understanding their needs, there will also be lots of qualities he will be able to offer his children. These, however, will be more practical and about the things he is able to teach them and show them. Fathers are as important to children as mothers and both play a very significant role, albeit a very different role in some cases. The emotional and nurturing side of parenting is best left for the non-AS mother to deal with as she has a spontaneous and natural instinct for this. If the AS partner supports her and values her as the mother of his children, between the two of them, they will be able to offer their children a good and healthy upbringing.

Rule 11

Do not expect children to be able to achieve the same as you.

Conclusion

The key characteristic that I have observed in many of the AS men I have worked with is the strong desire they have to try to make their partner happy in order for the relationship to succeed. The effort they make often means coming out of their comfort zone and behaving in a way that may feel quite alien to their nature; this effort can leave them feeling mentally exhausted. Sadly, for some this effort goes unappreciated or is taken for granted due to Asperger's being 'invisible' and not obvious, as some physical disabilities are. One person can only do so much – a relationship requires both partners to make the effort to make each other happy. If a man feels he is the only one making the effort it may help to seek out support and advice about the situation in which he finds himself.

40

Do you have a list of what I can do to try to make her happy in our relationship?

Despite being one of the questions I am asked most frequently, I have saved this question till now as I wanted to offer it in the form of a list that will summarise many of the questions in this book. Of course it would be impossible to write a list that would be guaranteed to make all women happy in a relationship. There will be women, as there will be men, who decide they do not want to be happy and no amount of effort on their partner's part will make any difference to that.

If you are a man with AS, have taken the time to read this book, and tried to do the best you can to make things better and more harmonious with your partner, yet you still find your partner very unhappy or of a blaming inclination towards you, then as a couple you might need professional help. There is only so much any one person can do within a relationship, as it does involve two people, and requires both to work at 'dancing' to the same tune, otherwise one or other may find their foot trodden upon. You cannot make things work on your own or allow yourself to be abused in the process; all you can offer another is your best, which is why I have called it a 'Things that could help to make her happy' list.

THINGS THAT COULD HELP TO MAKE HER HAPPY

- Smile when you greet her.
- Compliment her on her looks, clothes or something she has done.
- Buy her flowers/chocolates/fruit/gifts.
- Buy and write a nice card to go with your gift.

- On special occasions always write a special message which includes telling her that you love her.

- Tell her you love her at least once a day.

- If she is crying or upset give her a hug without necessarily saying anything.

- Never presume a hug means sex.

- When you hug or kiss her, try not to think about anything else but her.

- Try not to interrupt her when she is talking to you.

- Try not to correct her if she mispronounces a word or uses the wrong word.

- Try not to correct her if she exaggerates when in company.

- Explain beforehand that you may at times have to be alone or leave the room.

- Find another way to express feelings if words are difficult for you to find.

- If you feel overloaded leave the situation and resist becoming reactive.

- Do not presume she is being critical; ask her first before assuming.

- If she asks for your opinion on something sensitive, suggest she asks a friend.

- Agree to a compromise on how much quality time you spend together.

- Limit the time you spend on the internet or with your special interest.

- Do not even begin to explore porn on the internet; you may soon be drawn in and displease her.

- Do not expect her to participate in your particular routines.

- Do not force your need for structure and inflexible plans on her or your family.

- If you collect things then agree to a limit on the space you can use for those things.

- Encourage her to spend time with friends and family, as it is a form of social and emotional food to her.

- Ask her to write down any errands or tasks she wants you to do.

- Do not be tempted to fix her problems unless she asks for your help.

- Sometimes she will just want you to listen and not try to solve anything.

- Give her your time and attention, making her feel close to you.

- Tell her you love her when you make love.

- If you have children, remember that they are the responsibility of both of you.

- Come to an agreement on how chores and childcare are divided between you.

- Try to have fun with the family and laugh with them.

- Check with her how your child is doing in respect of their ability to perform certain tasks or their mental processes.

- Do not alienate yourself from the family; find something you can share with them.

- Agree a time that you can share with the children, doing things together or sharing an interest.

- Believe and trust that she loves you; accept and thank her for being in your life.

41

Are AS/non-AS relationships ever successful?

I have answered many of the questions in this book with a yes *and* a no. This question, however, can be answered with a *yes*, as many AS/non-AS relationships are successful. For those that do not succeed the reason is often down to the complexities of people, rather than being anything to do with Asperger syndrome. AS only really comes into the equation if it is unknown, denied or unaccepted. As long as a couple can accept and understand that their relationship is affected by AS, and appreciate what this means for both of them and that neither is to blame, then the relationship has as much chance as any relationship of surviving and thriving. If it fails it is more likely to be because of the couple's individual personalities, their capacity to commit to a relationship and how the couple interact, communicate and work together.

I often remind couples that having AS will not make a person good, bad, nice or nasty. It will not determine whether they are faithful, honest or hardworking. The AS person, as with all people, will come with their own unique personality – being affected by AS, however, can exaggerate aspects of personality but it will not create them. For example, if a person is born with an introvert type of personality, having AS could mean they would be even more introverted; likewise if a person has a predisposition to be disorganised, having AS may make them even more so.

When a couple first come to see me it is often because they have discovered the possibility that one of them is affected by Asperger syndrome. This is a really critical time for the couple as both will be in a stage of transition as they accept what this means and how it will affect their relationship. Every person will be unique in how they deal with this and the changes they are prepared to make to their perception, communication and behaviour, and each will be faced with various choices as to how they manage this as individuals. However, the first choice the couple will have to make is whether they wish to continue together, or whether they feel they should part. This will obviously depend on many factors and often the choices can be narrowed down to three. They can decide to like it, lump it or leave it. It really is as simple as that, but it is not always the case that both people in the relationship will make the same choice. So let us look at each of the three options, which I will address in reverse order.

LEAVE IT

Sometimes, by the time a couple come to see me, they have been struggling for years. More often than not, it is at the stage in their relationship when their children are leaving home for university or have married and moved on. A couple find themselves back to being a couple again. Up until then they have been Mum and Dad and shared a very strong common denominator, that of the children, with their focus and attention having been upon bringing them up as best they possibly could.

Once the children leave, it will give the couple time to look at each other and think now what? They may reflect and consider what it is they actually share together or evaluate whether their partner is the person they want to spend the rest of their years with. Sometimes the conclusion they reach is no, they do not want to spend their lives with their partner, and will make the decision to end the relationship. In the case of AS/non-AS relationships I find it is more likely to be the female partner who comes to this decision. She may feel she no longer has the energy to continue or anything left to offer the relationship and even the discovery of AS will not make her change her mind.

Sometimes AS will be the reason the woman gives for leaving, which can feel very cruel and hard for the man to cope with. The only consolation I can offer in this case is that her leaving was likely to have been on the agenda anyway; maybe her feelings had changed and, although she might still care for her partner, she is no longer in love with him and her sense of commitment to him may have left her some time previously. I suggested back in my first book *The Other Half of Asperger Syndrome*, which was written primarily for women living with AS men, that she should base her decision to leave or not leave on the things her partner has control over, rather than the fact that he is affected by Asperger syndrome (Aston 2001, p.77).

It can be very hard for a man with AS to accept that the relationship is over and that they will no longer be together; this time of transition can be especially hard for him. If the decision is hers alone, he may protest strongly, perhaps even become quite depressed and despondent. Once he accepts the situation, though, he may move on quite quickly and rapidly revert to thinking solo. The majority of men I speak with state that they find living in a stress-free environment and not having to feel guilty about the time they spend on the things they enjoy works very well for them, once they have adjusted to the change.

Staying on a positive note, it is also possible to leave it and like it. I have mentioned in this book that some couples decide that although they do not feel they can remain living together in the same house, they do not want to give up on their relationship or each other. In these cases the couple's commitment to each other is quite strong and neither is looking to move on into another relationship.

The decision the couple often come to when they both share the need to remain a couple but to live in their own homes is to almost revert to the courtship stage of their relationship and they will, after moving apart, arrange to spend quality time together, while knowing they can both go back home to their own environments.

Living apart can allow each to peruse their own interests and pastimes. For him that is often his special interest or his work, for her it is often the broadening of her social circle and spending more time with friends. It will be down to each to decide what works for them, while maintaining a level of quality time to spend together.

LUMP IT

For some men and women, however, there is not enough love and commitment and they may have reached a point where the personality clashes between them are so strong that they do not feel they share any common ground at all. If neither in this sad situation is prepared to move on or will accept the relationship is over or that leaving the relationship is an option open to them, sadly these couples will find themselves in the 'lump it' situation.

This can become a life of existing within the relationship, not one of living and enjoying. Couples who make this decision may soon find themselves feeling trapped, unhappy and lonely. Unfortunately, though, if the personality types of the couple are not compatible and the differences between them are great, 'lump it' may feel like the only choice available to them. 'Lump it' is not good for anyone and if there are children involved, having parents that are unhappy both with each other and with their situation will not create a healthy environment for those children to grow and develop in.

I have seen partners on both sides suffer when 'lump it' has been chosen. In some cases it is she who is the one who feels she is trapped and that may be because of her financial dependence upon him, religious commitments or the belief that children need two parents to thrive. Two happy parents living separately can be more beneficial to a child than two parents staying together in an abusive or argumentative relationship.

If one partner in a relationship is abusive, then the other really has to weigh up whether the benefits of staying outweigh the abuse they are experiencing. If their partner is treating them in a way that is physically, verbally or financially abusive and either they or the children are suffering because of this, then it is imperative that the couple seek help. No one has to suffer in silence and the danger of staying silent in an abusive relationship is that it can be seen to justify the abuse and make it acceptable. It is not acceptable and no man, woman or child should be made to suffer at the hands of another.

I found in my original research that men with AS will often stay in a relationship that is abusive rather than leave and in some cases not even protest against the abuse. Part of the reason for this is that their fear of change or confrontation is so great they will go to any lengths to avoid it. The men who are most likely to find themselves in this situation will undoubtedly belong to the passive group of men I see affected by AS. These men rarely have an aggressive streak in their body; their fear of confrontation, shouting and any form of anger may dominate their lives. If they have to part with their money to pacify the situation and avoid their partner getting angry then they will. Some men have tolerated being physically attacked and verbally abused, not disclosing their unhappiness to anyone. I find with men it is often the emotional abuse, rather than the physical abuse, that has the greater detrimental effect. Abuse is unacceptable in any relationship whether it is the man or the woman or both who are perpetrators, and I advise anyone in an abusive relationship to seek professional help and advice.

LIKE IT

Now we come to the best option of all, and the one I find presents itself most often. 'Like it' is by far the best alternative; it will mean that AS has been accepted and the couple will both learn together about what that means and will be working to develop an understanding of each other that is better than they ever shared before.

Both will be changing and that change will be quite different for both of them. For her she will find her communication style changes as she learns to talk to him in a logical language that he can understand, she will also be making it safe for him to be open and express himself, she will no longer have unrealistic expectations of him, she will understand that he will not always get it right and, yes, she will have to learn to absolutely spell out for him how she feels and what she wants him to do.

She will be learning to love him for who he is and to accept the different ways in which he expresses his love for her. Although this might not always be how she wanted or expected it to be, she will acknowledge that this is his way of expressing his love. She will lose her anger as she realises that this is a useless emotion which will render him unable to function or communicate. She will learn to live a life in which she takes responsibility for herself and feeds her emotional needs through friends where he is unable to.

She will be learning to live a life that will offer her freedom of thought, and a relationship that will allow her to maintain her autonomy and not question her trust. She will learn to love him for his mind and enjoy the interesting conversations that she can share with him, the many things he knows about, and to share his world along with his unique view of it. Men with AS do have a lot to offer but what they offer can only be appreciated if the time is taken to understand and accept the way they are.

For him, to be in 'like it' is quite different as the majority of men that I see only voice one requirement in the relationship and that is for her to be happy. So many men ask me 'How can I make her happy?' That is it in a nutshell; if she is happy then they state they are happy. In Question 40 I put together a whole list of the things he can do to help make his partner happier and if he can make this effort then his efforts should be well received and appreciated. The majority of men with AS do not want arguments and confrontations, neither do they want her to need him for her emotional support and are all too happy if she can get this need met by a close friend or a personal interest or hobby instead. A man with AS does not want to participate in mind games by having to guess what she wants; he wants a partner to be open, honest and say what she means; stay even tempered and predictable; allow him to have space to be alone or pursue his interest and to respect and love him.

That's it, and in return he will love her, stay committed for life and will be unlikely to stray or be a womaniser. She will not be chasing him out of the pub. She will have a partner who will, in most cases, work hard and be successful and will support her and his family financially. If he enjoys DIY, all the jobs in the house will be done to perfection (even if they take a while to complete!).

Both will have qualities that they can offer each other; if their personalities work together and the love and commitment they share for each other is strong, then there is a very good chance that the relationship will work and it will work well.

Rule 12

AS/non-AS relationships can work well
as long as both partners can accept
the differences between them.

References

Aston, M. (2001) *The Other Half of Asperger Syndrome*. London: National Autistic Society.

Aston, M. (2003) *Aspergers in Love: Practical Advice and Activities for Couples and Counsellors*. London: Jessica Kingsley Publishers.

Aston, M. (2008) *The Asperger Couple's Workbook: Practical Advice and Activities for Couples and Counsellors*. London: Jessica Kingsley Publishers.

Attwood, T. (2007) *The Complete Guide to Asperger's Syndrome*. London: Jessica Kingsley Publishers.

Baron-Cohen, S. (2003) *The Essential Difference*. London: Allen Lane.

Baron-Cohen, S., Wheelwright, S., Stott, C., Bolton, P. and Goodyer, I. (1997) 'Is there a link between engineering and autism?' *Autism 1*, 101–109.

Baron-Cohen, S., Wheelwright, S., Hill, J., Raste, Y. and Plumb, I. (2001) 'The "Reading the Mind in the Eyes" test. Revised version: A study with normal adults, and adults with Asperger syndrome or high-functioning autism.' *Journal of Child Psychiatry and Psychiatry 42*, 241–252.

Centers for Disease Control and Prevention (2012) 'Autism Spectrum Disorders (ASDs).' Available at www.cdc.gov/ncbddd/autism/index.html, accessed on 12 June 2012.

Hamann, S., Herman, R.A., Nolan, C.L. and Wallen, K. (2004) 'Men and women differ in amygdala response to visual sexual stimuli.' *Nature Neuroscience 7*, 411–416.

Happe, F. and Frith, U. (1995) 'Theory of Mind in Autism.' In E. Schopler and G.B. Mesibov (eds) *Learning and Cognition in Autism*. New York: Plenum Press.

Hill, E., Berthoz, S. and Frith, U. (2004) 'Brief report: cognitive processing of own emotions in individuals with autistic spectrum disorder and in their relatives.' *Journal of Autism and Developmental Disorders 34*, 2, 229–235.

Holliday Willey, L. and Attwood, T. (2000) *Asperger's Syndrome – Crossing the Bridge* [video]. London: Jessica Kingsley Publishers.

Jones, W., Carr, K. and Klin, A. (2008) 'Absence of preferential looking to the eyes of approaching adults predicts level of social disability in 2-year-old toddlers with autism spectrum disorder.' *Archives of General Psychiatry 65*, 8, 946–954.

Ozonoff, S., Roger, S.J. and Pennington, B.F. (1991) 'Asperger's syndrome: evidence of an empirical distinction from high-functioning autism.' *Journal of Child Psychology and Psychiatry 32*, 1107–1122.

Parker, J.D.A., Taylor, G.J. and Bagby, R.M. (2001) 'The relationship between emotional intelligence and alexithymia.' *Journal of Personality and Individual Differences 30*, 107–115.

Pease, A. and Pease, B. (2001) *Why Men Don't Listen and Women Can't Read Maps*. London: Orion.

Then, D. (1999) *Women Who Stay With Men Who Stray: Coping With the Realities of Infidelity*. New York: Hyperion Books.